Jossey-Bass Teacher

Jossey-Bass Teacher provides educators with practical knowledge and tools to create a positive and lifelong impact on student learning. We offer classroom-tested and research-based teaching resources for a variety of grade levels and subject areas. Whether you are an aspiring, new, or veteran teacher, we want to help you make every teaching day your best.

From ready-to-use classroom activities to the latest teaching framework, our value-packed books provide insightful, practical, and comprehensive materials on the topics that matter most to K–12 teachers. We hope to become your trusted source for the best ideas from the most experienced and respected experts in the field.

Digital Learning

Strengthening and Assessing 21st Century Skills

Ferdi Serim

Foreword by Monica Beglau

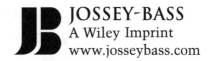

JOSSEY-BASS
A Wiley Imprint
www.josseybass.com

Published by Jossey-Bass
A Wiley Imprint
One Montgomery Street, Suite 1200, San Francisco, CA 94104-4594—www.josseybass.com

Jossey-Bass books and products are available through most bookstores. To contact Jossey-Bass directly call our Customer Care Department within the U.S. at 800-956-7739, outside the U.S. at 317-572-3986, or fax 317-572-4002.

Wiley publishes in a variety of print and electronic formats and by print-on-demand. Some material included with standard print versions of this book may not be included in e-books or in print-on-demand. If this book refers to media such as a CD or DVD that is not included in the version you purchased, you may download this material at **http://booksupport.wiley.com**. For more information about Wiley products, visit **www.wiley.com**.

Library of Congress Cataloging-in-Publication Data

Serim, Ferdi.
    Digital learning : strengthening and assessing 21st century skills, grades 5–8 / Ferdi Serim. –
1st ed.
        p. cm. – (Jossey-Bass teacher)
    Includes bibliographical references and index.
    ISBN 978-1-118-00233-9 (pbk.), 978-1-118-13105-3 (ebk.), 978-1-118-13106-0 (ebk.),
978-1-118-13107-7 (ebk.)
    1. Educational technology.   2. Technological literacy.   I. Title.
    LB1028.3.S4145 2012
    371.33–dc23
                                        2011028167

Printed in the United States of America

FIRST EDITION

PB Printing   10 9 8 7 6 5 4 3 2 1

About the Author

Ferdi Serim helps people become more effective in "real life" by incorporating the power of digital learning communities focused on talent development. He has worked in many venues: as a board member of the International Society for Technology in Education (ISTE); the EdTech director of the New Mexico Public Education Department, director of Reading First, program manager for Literacy, Technology & Standards; a board member of the Consortium for School Networking (CoSN), Innovate+Educate, and Education360; a director of the Online Internet Institute (OII); and as an associate of the David Thornburg Center for Professional Development. Ferdi pioneered the use of the Internet to improve learning, developing one of the first online professional development projects funded by the National Science Foundation. He managed annual investments of $12 million in educational technology for the State of New Mexico; he also managed the standards team responsible for moving New Mexico to A ratings for the quality of its academic standards. Ferdi has worked with leading national experts, including Dr. Robert Marzano, to develop online courses that advance understanding of standards-based assessment, instruction, and grading, to help educators prepare for adoption of the Common Core State Standards. He currently consults with leading organizations, districts, and ministries of education focused on transforming learning. He is the author of three books: *NetLearning: Why Teachers Use the Internet; From Computers to Community: Unlocking the Potentials of the Wired Classroom;* and *Information Technology for Learning: No School Left Behind.* Ferdi is also a jazz musician.

Ferdi has walked the talk: his students' Internet achievements are documented in *Scientific American,* the *Los Angeles Times,* the Learning Channel, and other media. He presents at numerous state, regional, and international conferences, and conducts staff development workshops and seminars for parents, teachers, school administrators, and others involved in systemic school reform, including the U.S. Department of Education, the National Science Foundation, Los Alamos National Labs, the Milken Exchange on Educational Technology, the Singapore and Malaysia ministries of education, and others. Ferdi's favorite credential, however, comes from Dizzy Gillespie, who said he's a "pretty good drummer."

Nearly a century ago, H. G. Wells observed, "Human history becomes more and more a race between education and catastrophe." The focus of history is often on the contestants in conflict, with victory on the battlefield followed by victory of the narrative. If we were to declare a war on ignorance, who would be the foe? For there are at least two kinds of ignorance: the kind caused by lack of exposure, so that people act without being aware of the choices they could make to improve their situation; there is also the kind where people erect barriers to prevent changes, believing that they can proceed as they always have, enjoying the benefits of an often imaginary security. This work is dedicated to the peaceful warriors working every day to roll back the veils of ignorance. In my mind, the role model for such a remarkable human being is Dr. Margot Ely, who opened my horizons beyond science and music to savor the wonders of all human invention, tradition, and culture. I was a fifth grader at the time. She is why I am an educator and the reason I can extend this dedication more widely.

This book is dedicated to those who learn, relentlessly. When asked why he robbed banks, John Dillinger replied "because that's where the money is." Although not all learning takes place in school, for people who are addicted to the joy of watching the lights go on in the learner's eyes when a new discovery or breakthrough happens, being a teacher greatly increases one's exposure to such moments. If you are a teacher who gets turned on by learning, this book is dedicated to you.

It is dedicated to those who help others learn, relentlessly. Some people who are motivated by learning are not satisfied keeping it to themselves. These individuals go out of their way to challenge and support the people they care about to rise to their highest levels, and the people they care about are not only their students but also their coworkers, families, and neighbors. If you see helping learners as dharma, this book is dedicated to you.

It is dedicated to those who discover and share new ways to learn, relentlessly. As Margaret Riel has stated, our role is to make our students more powerful versions of themselves. Such progress doesn't happen by chance, but rather from deliberate study and reflection. If you take time to keep up with the wealth of discoveries about how humans learn, about the conditions and practices that most powerfully extend learning so that it becomes the birthright of every individual, this book is dedicated to you.

I'm grateful to my ancestors, both in Turkey and in the United States; to my teachers (in school, in music, and in life); and to my family for supporting all three aspects of my journey. Although "rolling back the veils of ignorance" may sometimes seem a Sisyphean task, the true joy of sharing this work transcends any dues paid along the way. This book is dedicated to all of us, as partners in the journey.

Acknowledgments

The process by which this book came into your hands is unusual, and is itself a journey into project-based learning. In 2003, I realized that progress in extending the benefits of digital learning as a right for all students would be blocked unless and until we had ways of assessing what was then the relatively new idea called "21st century skills." The measurement mania was already creating a hyperfocus on what is tested, marginalizing development of key capabilities whose growth could not be strengthened until they could be observed. This became my project.

The first venue in which I explored these implications was provided by Keith Kreuger and the Consortium for School Networking (CoSN). That year, I keynoted the CoSN annual conference and outlined the principles that inform this work. These principles were developed within an informal community of learning pioneers, many of whom appear in this book and the accompanying DVD: Chris Dede, Margaret Riel, David Thornburg, and Doug Johnson are all superstars in their respective fields; they have generously guided and shaped my development for decades. Over the past eight years, our conversations have sharpened the focus, deepened the thinking, and extended the reach of what is now called the Digital Learning Process.

The challenge of designing an approach to assessing 21st century skills without the baggage of earlier centuries' limited view and understandings of learning is significant. Once again, I was fortunate to draw on immense insights of key leaders. Robert Marzano has significantly advanced our profession's grasp of applying research into practice, including moving into standards-based instruction and grading. During the two years I was privileged to work on developing an online course based on his video presentations, the power of his body of work and the commitment of hundreds of districts who have taken up his challenge to create systemic transformation have changed and improved my thinking on these topics.

The work of Helen Barrett is similarly influential. Helen developed the formulation for e-portfolios that shapes today's practice. My work on the Digital Learning Process has benefited from the research and recommendations she continues to share with the field. As I note elsewhere in this book, Helen teaches us that Evidence = Artifact + Reflection + Validation. This insight allowed the development of the project maps you will learn about; they are the digital artifacts that allow teachers and students to use digital communications and collaboration tools to reflect on the learning, by allowing the thinking processes to become visible.

Validation is provided by the largest global enterprise focused on the advancement of education. Although it is true that once as a board member I had the temerity to suggest renaming the group Innovative Systems for Transforming Education, ISTE (the International Society for Technology in Education) has been doing just fine for its first thirty years and will likely continue to do so with its original name. My esteemed colleagues and dear friends at ISTE are like my extended family, and without the sustained encouragement and support I've enjoyed from Don Knezek, Leslie Conery, Lynn Nolan, Jayne James, and Jessica Medaille, the NETS, though they would still be powerful, might not be part of my DNA. Similarly, the leadership of the three ISTE board presidents I was privileged to serve has raised the standards by which I measure any leader: Kurt Steinhaus, Trina Davis, and Helen Padgett have each inspired me to stretch beyond limits each and every day.

In one way, I am glad this process has taken nearly a decade, because it was toward the end that I encountered some of the most powerful work and ideas. Although Judy Harris's seminal work in telementoring changed the practice of online educators for decades, her latest work in researching, cataloging, and organizing learning activities that effectively use technology in service of academic goals has added immensely to this work. Judy's generosity in helping me dive deeper and beyond a superficial grasp of the TPACK system has been invaluable.

The contributions of Tina Rooks, with regard to twenty-first-century assessments, and Kari Stubbs, on project-based learning, greatly strengthened the processes you'll learn about in this book. Rita Oates's tireless quest to boost the power of what students and teachers can accomplish through global collaboration has provided another great improvement to the digital educator's tool kit.

In 2007, I met Dave Master, who was keynoting the NSBA Technology and Learning conference in Nashville, a fateful meeting that has caused convergence of our lives and work. Dave created the largest, most successful online coaching and mentoring network in the United States by building a social network for learning, years before the words "social" and "network" appeared next to one another and Facebook had even been dreamed of. My focus on building online communities for professional development had begun with an NSF project in 1995, so the fit was natural. What has emerged most powerfully is surprisingly not about the technology but instead about looking at student work. By vastly improving the rigor and authenticity of student challenges and by carefully examining both what students produce and the processes they use, teachers can deepen and accelerate learning. Dave provided independent validation that these concepts not only work but work at scale. Dave's impact and influence in developing implementation models for social learning that drive this entire process can't be overstated.

Ubuntu is a Swahili word that means "I am who I am because of who we are together," and it captures the ethos of the open education resource movement. The constellations of luminaries shaping and leading the efforts to improve education cover the skies. I particularly acknowledge Tom Carroll, Kathleen Fulton, and Karen Smith of the National Commission on Teaching and America's Future (NCTAF) and their colleague Paul Resta (University of Texas at Austin) for allowing me to join in their work on redefining teacher education and developing powerful models that provide viable alternatives to allow us to "build the schools we need" instead of "fixing" the schools we have. Similarly, the opportunity to participate in the work that Tom Ryan, Brian Ormand, Jamai Blivin, and industry supporters of Innovate+Educate are doing to develop solid models for "transforming education from the inside out" has provided an unequalled "living laboratory" for the research and development of my ideas.

None of what you are about to experience would have been produced without the special gifts and talents of two organizations that took my work and supported its transformation into product. Alvin Crawford of Knowledge Delivery Systems invested in the filming of my presentations and interviews to make the Digital Learning Process a part of the innovative educational technology online courses that launched FETC University and have been widely used by educators nationwide. Lesley Iura of Jossey-Bass/Wiley believed in this project so that it could become the book you hold now. The quality, clarity, and cogency you encounter is the result of having one of the best editors in publishing at the helm. I was elated when I learned that Kate Bradford would be guiding this book through the process, and my gratitude and respect for her acumen has grown every day, as has my appreciation for Nana Twumasi's incredible ability to bring order to chaos and calendars.

Finally, I thank you, for your willingness to consider and explore innovations that require you, and everyone you work with (students, parents, peers, and school leaders), to examine everything we do through a very rigorous lens: if what we do is helping kids prepare for a future filled with expanded opportunity, we will continue to do it; if not, we won't, and we will remove any obstacle that stands in the way. This commitment unavoidably puts us in the path of conflict and controversy, as old and new worlds collide. Until recently, the path of least resistance was "business as usual," but it is becoming clearer every day that we can no longer afford (on any level) to sustain practices that don't work. I acknowledge and salute your efforts to build the schools we need, starting now!

Contents

Foreword by Monica M. Beglau   xv

Preface: Digital Age Learning Requires Digital Age Skills   xvii

1   **Digital Age Learning: Why Now? Why Me?**   1

2   **Rethinking Best Practices and Digital Age Learning**   23

3   **The Digital Learning Process**   33

4   ***Do* Try This at Home! Checking Your Digital Age Teaching and Learning Tool Kit**   53

5   **Eyes on the Prize!**   58

6   **Walking the Talk: Evolving Your Practice with NETS for Teachers**   141

Appendix A: Connect Your Classroom and Real Life: Career Clusters   156

Appendix B: Multidisciplinary Project: Our Community Fifty Years from Now   165

Appendix C: How to Use the DVD   169

Notes   174

Index   176

DVD Contents

1   **English Projects**

    English 01 Who's Selling Us Now?

    English 02 Who's Telling the Truth? Whose Truth Is Being Told?

    English 03 Web Reader's Guide

    English 04 Learning to Swim in a Sea of Data

    English 05 Literature Circles Meet Web 2.0

2   **Math Projects**

    Math 01 Same Problems, Different Answers?

    Math 02 How to Lie with Statistics

    Math 03 Making Math Meaning, in Teams

    Math 04 Down the Drain

    Math 05 Redesign Your School in Green

3   **Science Projects**

    Science 01 Do You Hear What I Hear?

    Science 02 Troubled Waters

    Science 03 On Solid Ground?

    Science 04 If Habitats Could Talk

    Science 05 Be Earth's Biographer

4   **Geography Projects**

    Geography 01 Nominate Local Landmarks

    Geography 02 Map Your Community!

    Geography 03 Lands Like Ours

    Geography 04 Invent to Save Lives!

    Geography 05 Inform Your Local Leaders

5 Resources

Digital Learning Trends Template (spreadsheet)

Digital Learning Trends Sample (spreadsheet)

PrePost NETS S Assessment

TPACK Activity Types (spreadsheet)

Notes (DVD version in Word)

6 Video Clips

1 Chris Dede Interviews
   1 Intro Chris Dede.mov
   2 Chris Dede—Vision.mov
   3 Chris Dede—Team Learning.mov
   4 Chris Dede—Connected Teaching Model.mov

2 David Thornburg Interviews
   1 David Thornburg—Online Learning.mov
   2 David Thornburg Creativity.mov
   3 David Thornburg Math Projects.mov
   4 David Thornburg Science and Career Clusters.mov
   5 David Thornburg STEM.mov

3 Digital Learning and TPACK Activity Types

4 Doug Johnson Interview

5 Kari Stubbs Interview

6 Margaret Riel Interview

7 MultiDisciplinary Project Videos

8 Tina Rooks Interviews

Foreword

In this articulate and practical guide to digital learning, Ferdi Serim provides a solid bridge that any educator can use to bravely transition into the future of education. In my forty years as a special educator, principal, and university academic professional, I have personally witnessed the power of technology and digital learning. In the 1980s, a child in my special education classroom who was unable to speak and had difficulty using sign language due to a neurological impairment was given one of the first digital communication devices available. For the first time in his young life, he had a voice. I was eager to know what his first words would be. Perhaps he would want to ask for his favorite food or for his favorite television show. With a broad smile, he made it clear what he wanted to say: he wanted to be able to call his dog, just like any other seven-year-old boy. Technology transformed his silent world into one of two-way communication, choice, and the power to reach out to something very important in his life.

Working with the eMINTS (enhancing Missouri's Instructional Networked Teaching Strategies) programs since 1999 has provided me with opportunities to observe and understand elements that are essential to helping learners gain personal mastery of complex content and concepts while developing character traits needed for success. The eMINTS National Center is a nonprofit organization at the University of Missouri providing research-based comprehensive professional development programs to educators since 1999. (See http: www.emints.org). In eMINTS classrooms, teachers and students alike become intrepid explorers, not only discovering content and concepts but also uncovering how they learn best and what talents others in their classroom communities possess. The student who was too shy to contribute to classroom discussions demonstrates an amazing capacity to design graphic representations. The student who was always in trouble finds that his abilities to problem-solve technical challenges gains him newfound respect among his classmates. The student who is a natural leader grows even more by learning how to distribute her leadership to create a strong working team.

The transformations that technology and digital learning offer to all learners can be profound and powerful in their impact. Digital learning can give teachers and students a view of the world and access to new ideas that can truly inspire their development of the voices we need to shape our future world.

Among the most critical elements uncovered by eMINTS through years of careful research is the need for educators to have both a strong foundation in the content area they are teaching and fluency in using technology. Equally important, however, is for teachers to be nurtured in their unquenchable curiosity about how to make learning more exciting and interesting to their students. These are precisely the elements that Ferdi brings home in practical and thorough examples in this book. Teachers, library media specialists, principals, curriculum coordinators, and technology specialists will all find insights into digital learning that can help them function at higher levels individually and as a team.

Ferdi Serim brings a passion to his work, offering educators an introduction to digital learning as well as a friendly support system to jump-start the planning that must precede the best project-based digital learning experiences. His discussion of digital technology tools makes it easy to imagine how they might be employed to create powerful learning adventures, regardless of the quantity of digital tools available in any given classroom. Focusing on such skills as creativity and collaboration in the multitude of rich examples discussed throughout the book, Ferdi offers educators a gentle push that might be needed to help them think more creatively themselves and collaborate more with their peers to examine their teaching. His probing questions and humorous observations challenge readers to reimagine their classrooms and their teaching so that they provide their students with a depth of knowledge and the social skills needed to succeed throughout their lives.

As a talented storyteller who weaves the sights and sounds of his multicultural experiences into his work, Ferdi offers readers realistic and touching glimpses into how classrooms might look and sound if digital learning were fully deployed. By highlighting the International Society for Technology in Education's (ISTE) National Educational Technology Standards for students (NETS-S) and for teachers (NETS-T), he helps educators see themselves as learners and helps them understand how their lifelong learning habits can serve as models for their students. Ferdi has drawn on his best stories of courage to create engaging scenarios that bring digital learning to life.

I hope that you enjoy thinking about and trying some of the stimulating ideas that Ferdi brings to light in this book. The future begins now . . .

Monica M. Beglau, EdD
Executive Director
eMINTS National Center
University of Missouri

Preface
Digital Age Learning Requires Digital Age Skills

For too long, the goal of connecting classroom learning with real-life relevance has seemed beyond our grasp, with the vast potentials of digital age learning taking root in only a relative handful of pioneering educators' learning environments. I've written this book to provide a practical bridge that any educator can use to cross into the future of learning.

Your exploration of the intersection of core subjects and digital age learning is designed to awaken your curiosity and anchor your understanding in a solid foundation. Traditionally, what and how (and whether) students are thinking is revealed too late, after testing shows whether they "got the answer right." By using the International Society for Technology in Education (ISTE) National Educational Technology Standards for Students (NETS-S) to learn *what to look for,* and graphic organizers to *see what they're thinking as they are learning,* we gain the ability to see into what had previously been a "black box" process. In each chapter, we'll explore how core content subject-area knowledge provides a foundation for reaching ever higher into the more sophisticated and powerful applications of learning demanded by life in the 21st century.

Each of the suggested project-based learning examples in Chapter Five (in language arts, mathematics, science, and geography) can be used successfully as a stand-alone unit, but are even more effective when approached in a cross-disciplinary way. At the elementary level, this is natural, as the same person typically teaches each subject. As we go up through the middle school and high school levels, the necessity of working with our colleagues in a strong and collaborative way poses unique challenges. We who have tried it can testify that the rewards are worth the effort!

Therefore, another purpose of this book is to provide teachers in each discipline with a common language and approach for building and strengthening these vital collaborative relationships. By framing instruction within the language of the ISTE NETS, we can begin to see the common threads of our lessons, regardless of subject matter. By framing assessment within the format of graphical organizers, we find a common method for "seeing how and what students are thinking," which is the only way to assess the cognitive development on which mastery of digital age learning skills depends.

Ten Thousand Hours of Practice, Mastery, and Us

I have been a teacher for thirty-seven years. I have been a musician for fifty years. This gives me a different perspective on the rule stating that it takes ten thousand hours of practice to attain expert-level performance than I had when I was in my twenties. Here's the gist of it: we are all practicing all the time, every day. That's why our habits are so strong. When we look at the list of our behaviors that have ten thousand hours or more of practice behind them, and compare that list with our aspirations, the mystery about why things are as they are evaporates.

If you spend half of every workday focusing on mastering a new set of skills or behaviors, given a two-thousand-hour work year, you can expect your practice odometer to move into five digits at the decade mark. When I began teaching in Newark, New Jersey, in 1973, I faced a choice and made a prayer. I had to decide whether to be a musician or a music teacher. I realized that the way things were going, by the time I mastered my instrument, it was likely that the yearly decline in listening skills and audiences for live music would leave no one to play for, so I decided I'd better start growing those listeners. I put up this prayer: at the end of ten years, please don't let me be one of those music teachers who can teach but who can no longer play.

About ten years later, I was on the bandstand with Dizzy Gillespie, and for several years after that had the honor of teaching young musicians to play his charts. It took my working with them for three to four months as a jazz artist in residence to prepare them to acceptable levels, and once ready, Dizzy would come into town to play a community concert with the kids. We'd raise enough money from that one show to fund a series of jazz master concerts, each of which included a master class with the guest artist, and we did this several times throughout the Delaware Valley region in the 1980s.

Fast forward to 1990. By then, I'd worked for twelve thousand hours as a program data manager for two different engineering companies (which is the source of my technology chops) and discovered I could not find anyone to hire who could think with his or her computer. Interviewing candidates for three months in the Philadelphia area, I found plenty who could operate sophisticated programs and write reams of ingenious code, but no one who wasn't stopped dead when I pointed to the screen and asked four words: "What does it mean?" At that point I decided that if I couldn't hire them, I'd better grow them, and returned to teaching, this time as a computer teacher.

Within the first year, I realized that the kids weren't the problem. They did amazing things, provided the opportunity and support. Our students participated in early (pre–World Wide Web) groundbreaking uses of the Internet that got them featured in *Scientific American,* the *Los Angeles Times,* and on the Learning Channel without ever leaving our classroom in New Jersey. But in classrooms next door, it was business as usual, with all the answers to the questions in the back of the book. I realized that teachers needed support and permission to seize opportunities to transform the learning that takes place in their classrooms, and not much about that has changed since.

It has now been about twenty years since I added transforming opportunities for learning through professional development to my practice, and that odometer keeps turning. I may not hit six digits, but that odometer won't stop until I do. The key is in taking the care to set up situations where it is likely that something useful will be learned. After a while, you begin to recognize the signs, to get a sense of when you're entering an interaction where new understandings are being revealed. Always stay on the lookout for such moments, when you realize you're likely to learn something from what you're doing.

There really is no mystery; this technique has long been known as reflective practice. It's what turns hours of habit reinforcement into opportunities to rise to new levels of mastery. Sometimes these moments arrive when you encounter people who have a special combination of gifts: they not only have developed rich and deep understandings and found powerful ways to share and express them but also are willing to help your advancement. I've been fortunate to have as such friends and mentors Chris Dede, Margaret Riel, David Thornburg, and Doug Johnson. In musician terms, they "sat in" on the online course that accompanies this book, adding remarkable insights and perspectives (which are shared throughout the book and on the accompanying DVD) to reinforce the collaborative aspect of knowledge building within an expert-informed community of practice.

Now I'll share with you something you may not know. The words you're reading now have been, are being, or will be read by others in several different situations. Some are reading this book as part of an online course, putting in forty-five hours (equivalent to three grad credits) toward their ten thousand hours of mastery. Others are reading it as members of a collaborative team in their school or district, as part of the district's investment in the strategic management of human capital. Still others have seen or participated in a webinar or read a blog post or (my favorite) had a friend tell them about the processes shared in this book, and were drawn in by something that resonated. Whatever the prompt that brings you to this process, one of the central tenets of digital learning is that "none of us is as smart as all of us" and that the readers of this book represent a "we" whose potential is unlocked when we decide to learn together.

More Than a Book?

What we're building is an evidence-based, expert-informed community of practice (I dare you to turn that into an acronym!) in which every hour you invest toward your ten thousand is amplified by the interactions with similarly focused colleagues. The kind of digital learning described in this book has multiple on-ramps, tailored to diverse needs and situations. You will always find "up to the moment" additions at the Digital Learning Process website: http://digitallearningprocess.net/. Here are some unifying characteristics you'll notice when you come aboard:

Instead of puzzled looks or stunned silence, you'll get answers from colleagues like

- Here's what I need to learn and why
- Here's how I'll be using it, and what I aim to gain

People will come for various purposes:

- Some plan to lead others through this course, after completion.
- Some plan to coach a site-based study group.
- Some plan to coach an online study group.

People will organize into a system of cascading mentorship (in which you are simultaneously a protégé of someone more advanced and the mentor for someone who's trying to learn something you recently mastered), through statements like these:

- Here's the instructional context where I'll apply what I learn.
- These are the roles I've played and that I am good at and am willing to play here.
- This is the role I want to prepare to play next.

People may not "know what they're doing," but they'll know what they're working on!

For most of the two decades that I've witnessed the extended labor attendant with the birth of the "technology integrated classroom," the discussion has centered on either-or questions: Is the socialization found in traditional brick-and-mortar classrooms better for students than online learning environments? Is direct instruction more effective than project-based learning? Is face-to-face learning preferable to online? The problem is in the questions: they force false choices that obscure the potential power of a model that blends both "real life" and online learning environments. We arrive at different answers and strategies when we seek to combine the best of each approach to meet the specific needs of each learner.

My view of the blended model is simple: because there is nothing that beats the immediacy and engagement of "real life" experience, let everything that can be done online or through technology be done that way (think research, skill development, drafting-revising-creating) so that precious face-to-face exchanges can be focused on interactions, coaching, and feedback. Because time and travel constraints limit the experiences we can bring into our physical classrooms, let technology bring those resources, relationships, and experiences that do work effectively in digital environments into our plans and projects. This is the essence of the blended model: finding the best mix of both to achieve a particular educational goal.

As we reach a tipping point where the transformation of education changes from Mission Impossible to Mission Inevitable, my fondest hope is that educators who employ the strategies that follow will embrace the opportunities to join blended-model communities to support one another's work.

Ferdi Serim
Santa Fe, New Mexico

Preface

Chapter 1

Digital Age Learning
Why Now? Why Me?

As educators, we live in two different worlds. Whether or not we have children of our own, we can sympathize with parents who receive a steady stream of reports lamenting that what students are required to do during the school day is not preparing them for real life. But when we go to work and put on our educator hats, we know that each day is packed to overflowing, making it impossible even to consider adding any new activities. Given this situation, it's a small wonder that so little has changed in the twenty years since computers entered our classrooms.

When we want to experience what life was like in colonial times, we can always visit the historical interpretive villages of Williamsburg or Plimoth Plantation. Too many classrooms could serve a similar role in preserving the instructional roles and goals of prior centuries.

The Digital Learning Process integrates instruction, performance, and assessment so that both the learner and teacher know what's been learned, what needs to be improved, and how to improve. This design heals the fractured nature of traditional approaches, which often break apart the natural process of learning into arbitrary and artificial acts that contribute little of value to guide continuous improvement on the part of the learner or the teacher. Instead, through engaging projects, learners develop 21st century skills by applying foundational core content skills to real-world challenges.

The Digital Learning Process provides a way out of the dilemma of whether to teach core subjects or 21st century skills. By incorporating tasks that include questions designed to cause students to think in 21st century ways and by providing a process for making this thinking visible for reflection by students and teachers, we make it possible to create and examine evidence of student thinking. As Helen Barrett has taught, Evidence = Artifacts + Reflection + Validation.[1]

The Digital Learning Process mirrors a key point in literacy development: at a certain stage, students move from *learning to read* to *reading to learn*. Similarly, *thinking about how we think* is a metacognitive skill that taps in to higher-order reasoning and enables us to explore and learn complex systems and issues.

In this book, I rely on the following leading resources for each topic. The goals come from the International Society for Technology in Education (ISTE) and its newly refreshed National Educational Technology Standards (NETS), which form the most widely used set of technology standards worldwide. We will examine both the student (NETS-S) and the teacher (NETS-T) versions, as only when teachers master both does the full range of digital learning become possible. The NETS-S and the symbols used to represent each are reproduced in their entirety here:

ISTE National Educational Technology Standards for Students (NETS-S)

1. Creativity and Innovation

Students demonstrate creative thinking, construct knowledge, and develop innovative products and processes using technology. Students:

A. apply existing knowledge to generate new ideas, products, or processes.

B. create original works as a means of personal or group expression.

C. use models and simulations to explore complex systems and issues.

D. identify trends and forecast possibilities.

2. Communication and Collaboration

Students use digital media and environments to communicate and work collaboratively, including at a distance, to support individual learning and contribute to the learning of others. Students:

A. interact, collaborate, and publish with peers, experts, or others employing a variety of digital environments and media.

B. communicate information and ideas effectively to multiple audiences using a variety of media and formats.

C. develop cultural understanding and global awareness by engaging with learners of other cultures.

D. contribute to project teams to produce original works or solve problems.

3. Research and Information Fluency

Students apply digital tools to gather, evaluate, and use information. Students:

A. plan strategies to guide inquiry.

B. locate, organize, analyze, evaluate, synthesize, and ethically use information from a variety of sources and media.

C. evaluate and select information sources and digital tools based on the appropriateness to specific tasks.

D. process data and report results.

4. Critical Thinking, Problem Solving, and Decision Making

Students use critical thinking skills to plan and conduct research, manage projects, solve problems, and make informed decisions using appropriate digital tools and resources. Students:

A. identify and define authentic problems and significant questions for investigation.

B. plan and manage activities to develop a solution or complete a project.

C. collect and analyze data to identify solutions and/or make informed decisions.

D. use multiple processes and diverse perspectives to explore alternative solutions.

5. Digital Citizenship

Students understand human, cultural, and societal issues related to technology and practice legal and ethical behavior. Students:

A. advocate and practice safe, legal, and responsible use of information and technology.

B. exhibit a positive attitude toward using technology that supports collaboration, learning, and productivity.

C. demonstrate personal responsibility for lifelong learning.

D. exhibit leadership for digital citizenship.

6. **Technology Operations and Concepts**

Students demonstrate a sound understanding of technology concepts, systems, and operations. Students:

A.   understand and use technology systems.

B.   select and use applications effectively and productively.

C.   troubleshoot systems and applications.

D.   transfer current knowledge to learning of new technologies.

The activities are adapted from the Partnership for 21st Century Skills Information and Communication Technologies (ICT) maps (http://www.p21.org/index.php?option=com_content&task=view&id=31&Itemid=33). Graphical organizers, available on the accompanying DVD, will allow you to use the ISTE NETS symbols for each of the six standards to assess and strengthen student learning.

The ICT maps have been developed for grades 4, 8, and 12. The activities in this book are intended to support students in grades 5 through 8. High school is a powerful setting for applying this process, as the current focus on Career and College Ready primes students for a deeper understanding of how well-developed digital age learning skills will widen their range of opportunities. But middle school is a powerful milestone, especially when one considers the requirements for all students to be technologically literate by eighth grade (as included in NCLB).

The single largest deficit among today's students is covered by the Critical Thinking, Problem Solving, and Decision Making standard. Students develop these skills only through use, and typical academic tasks neither develop nor reinforce the required habits of mind. This is why I've structured Digital Learning Projects as examples of the Digital Learning Process in action, so that meeting this deficit can become part of everyday life in your classroom. Each specific standards-based project unit integrates core subject content in contexts that require the use of 21st century skills. These projects are expressed as Digital Learning Project Maps that combine the goals, strategies, and resources you need in order to bring this type of learning to life in your classroom, and can be a most effective way of remediating this troublesome situation and reengaging your students through authentic, challenging tasks.

Andragogy—How (and Why) Adults Learn

Pedagogy has come to mean "how we teach," which in some cases is influenced by how students learn. However, contrasting how adults learn "in real life" and how we instruct in schools reveals profound differences. This divergence may be responsible for the growing tension between "school learning" and the difficulty employers report in finding school graduates who can meet the requirements for functioning at high levels in today's workplaces.

Andragogy is often described as a theory of how adults learn, but it actually refers to how humans learn, once they have passed the developmental point where they know the language, stories, and cultural norms of the society they inhabit. Once you can walk and talk, know nursery rhymes and folk tales, and get the jokes told in your neighborhood, advancing to andragogy is a good idea. By this definition, you may consider your students young adults.

The tenets of andragogy were originally developed in 1833 by a German educator, Alexander Kapp, as a theory of how "humans learn."[2] Andragogy was adapted into a theory of adult education by the American educator Malcolm Knowles, as shown in the following diagram that I've created as a graphical organizer.

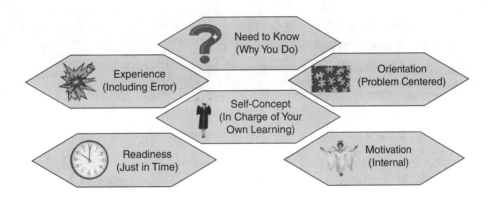

Throughout this book and on the accompanying website and DVD, I will use the following symbols as reminders or shorthand to connect the content with the andragogy element in question. Sometimes this will reinforce my reason for including a reading, activity, or resource. Other times it will be a prompt for you to reply within your community of practice.

Here's how andragogy shapes what you and your students will do in the Digital Learning Process, and how we will use the symbols in the book:

 1. People need to know the reason for learning something. At the introduction of each new topic, I will make explicit the connection between the new processes, tools, and tasks you're completing and how they expand your options. This prompt will also be used to indicate places where you should respond with your personal account of why you need to learn a topic or skill.

 2. Experience (including error) serves as the basis for learning activities. Another way of putting this is, "If you're not making any

mistakes, you're not trying hard enough to learn anything new." Allow, expect, and know how to use the learning opportunities error provides. Don't let errors go unnoticed or uncommented, but instead let errors prompt you to build to deeper understandings. Remember: many discoveries started out as mistakes.

Readiness (Just in Time)

3. People are most interested in learning subjects that have immediate relevance to their work and personal lives. Just-in-time learning (driven by the immediacy of the need to know) beats "just in case" (it may be on the test) every time, by providing a more specific connection to something you are trying to do but may not completely know how to do yet.

Orientation (Problem Centered)

4. Adults situate learning tasks as problem centered rather than content oriented (listing all the things it may be important to know about a topic). For example, there are many things you could learn about learning in the digital age, but what makes it into this book is what will help you solve the problem of enhancing your daily practice. The problem this book is trying to solve is how to simultaneously deepen students' learning of core content standards and of digital age skills.

Motivation (Internal)

5. People respond better to internal rather than external motivators. The professional satisfaction you'll derive from better preparing your students for expanded life opportunities outweighs the fame or fortune you're likely to earn for doing so.

Self-concept (In Charge of Your Own Learning)

6. People need to be responsible for their decisions with regard to education, including involvement in the planning and evaluation of their instruction. This is a unique characteristic of online learning, especially in a blended model. Many of you reading this book are taking the online course or have had experiences with other online professional development. The difference it makes when you are in charge (of pacing, depth, engagements, and providing feedback to peers, instructors, and designers) provides benefits you will want to extend to your students.

Let's practice. The problem of simultaneously deepening students' learning of core content standards and of digital age skills is accentuated when we take the pedagogy path instead of the andragogy path for professional development. That is why this book starts out with your need to know what comes next: it is important to understand that the types of learning that were once reserved for top performers (in school and society) in Ozzie and Harriet's day are now expected of everyone. College and Career Ready standards demand that everyone, for example, have sufficient abstract reasoning ability that he or she can complete Algebra I and II. The question "How will I use this in real life?" has shifted to "What kind of real-life opportunities open for me when I demonstrate mastery?" This is also why we look at both NETS-S and NETS-T.

Digital Learning Project Test Drive: *Who's Selling Us Now?*

 Taking a quick look at one Digital Learning Project gives you a concrete reference point for what follows, and you are encouraged to click on the links in the digital version of the book, which you'll find on the included DVD.

Who's Selling Us Now? is a project-based unit intended to get students to examine how their buying habits may be influenced without their knowledge, and to become aware of marketing efforts targeted at their considerable discretionary purchasing power.

Like all Digital Learning Projects, it is based on a Partnership for 21st Century Skills ICT map. Here's the original assignment: *Choose a variety of advertisements of products from favorite magazines, TV shows, or websites that are personally appealing. Analyze the techniques used by each advertisement to attract teen buyers.*

The project begins by directing students to a website produced by PBS: Frontline in support of a segment it aired called "The Merchants of Cool" (http://www.pbs.org/wgbh /pages/frontline/shows/cool/), which offers an in-depth, behind-the-scenes view of the multibillion-dollar industry that exists to shape teens' buying habits. In order to increase student engagement, in my project design I applied the principles of project-based learning (these will be elaborated on in later chapters). In order to place students at the center of their own learning, I expanded the definition of the task to include surveys of students to determine the degree to which the findings of "The Merchants of Cool" were present in the school community, to quantify and report on which media students were exposed to, and to assess their ability to identify techniques intended to make ads "personally appealing." Digital Learning Project Maps combine the desired core curriculum objectives and distribute activities across the relevant ISTE NETS as is most appropriate. In this case, the curricular focus is on the persuasive use of language and media, within English/Language Arts Common Core State Standards. (To download the standards, see http://www .corestandards.org/the-standards.)

If you've not been following discussions about "the Common Core" in the news, here is the background. The Common Core State Standards Initiative is a state-led effort coordinated by the National Governors Association Center for Best Practices and the Council of Chief State School Officers. It is a response to the fact that if the total number of state academic standards (calculated to be at least thirty-one hundred) were to be taught, it would require twenty-two years. Consolidation and alignment are required to bring this down to a workable number.

Developed in collaboration with teachers, school administrators, and experts, the Common Core State Standards form a clear and consistent framework to prepare our children for college and the workforce. These standards define the knowledge and skills students should acquire over the course of their K–12 education careers so that they will graduate high school able to succeed in entry-level, credit-bearing academic college courses and in workforce training programs. To learn more about these new standards, see http://www.corestandards.org/about-the-standards.

The Assessment Anchors clarify the standards assessed on state assessments and can be used by educators to help prepare their students for these tests. The anchor metaphor represents the unchanging connection that the Assessment Anchors have to the state assessment system and the curriculum and instructional practices in schools.

The "big idea" is that having fifty different sets of academic standards makes little sense and gets in the way of assuring that what students learn in one state is equivalent to what they learn in another. This has powerful implications for both prospective employers and for online learning. Aligning Digital Learning Project Maps with Common Core State Standards is an intentional decision to help teachers move in this direction with greater ease.

Specifically, in reviewing the Common Core for English/Language Arts, I identified the following standards as most relevant to the *Who's Selling Us Now?* project:

Grades 6–12 College and Career Readiness Anchor Standards for Reading

Integration of Knowledge and Ideas

7. Integrate and evaluate content presented in diverse formats and media, including visually and quantitatively, as well as in words.*

8. Delineate and evaluate the argument and specific claims in a text, including the validity of the reasoning as well as the relevance and sufficiency of the evidence.

9. Analyze how two or more texts address similar themes or topics in order to build knowledge or to compare the approaches the authors take.

*Please see "Research to Build Knowledge" in Writing and "Comprehension and Collaboration" in Speaking and Listening for additional standards relevant to gathering, assessing, and applying information from print and digital sources.

Students are challenged to produce a short video (under ninety seconds) as a public service announcement (PSA) that would convey their findings and reveal their mastery of the Integration of Knowledge and Ideas standards.

This project can be completed over several days in class or can be completed by student teams working online, outside of class, with weekly "check-ins" in class to review progress and share problem-solving strategies.

Here is how the six ISTE NETS contribute over the span of the project. It is important to note that the NETS are not linear but recursive. This means that over the course of the project, you and your students will return to them whenever necessary, as often as necessary. Please note: Research and Information Fluency is the heart of this particular project.

B. create original works as a means of personal or group expression.

Students create a PSA presenting the findings of their survey of advertising techniques that are directed toward teens in our community and offering suggestions on how to "avoid the bait."

B. communicate information and ideas effectively to multiple audiences using a variety of media and formats.

Students work in teams to choose the most important messages that need to be conveyed in their ninety-second PSAs.

B. locate, organize, analyze, evaluate, synthesize, and ethically use information from a variety of sources and media.

This standard includes media literacy and is therefore the heart of the project. The sheer volume of information that will be generated by student review of advertising will require strong skills in organizing and summarizing the data collected. This provides a perfect opportunity to teach effective strategies.

D. use multiple processes and diverse perspectives to explore alternative solutions.

Most advertising is subliminal, designed to do its work "under the radar," so students for whom a particular ad is less successful are more likely to see what's going on. In order to begin to see the patterns, we need to combine information from multiple sources to identify the techniques used by each advertisement to attract teen buyers.

B. exhibit a positive attitude toward using technology that supports collaboration, learning, and productivity.

Collaborative learning and development of effective presentations of what's been learned can be of great benefit to students as well as parents. When both audiences become aware of the marketing strategies used to drive purchases of the largest group of consumers with the most disposable income (teens), important conversations can begin both at school and at home.

D. transfer current knowledge to learning of new technologies.

Creating a PSA video may be new to many students (and teachers), so building on prior knowledge (of audio recording, building PowerPoints, writing scripts, taking digital photographs, and so on) is an important strategy. Equally important is locating effective online tutorials!

Your Road Map to Success with Digital Age Learning

When Noah heard "Build an ark!" he didn't start designing a hovercraft. Instead, he built what could be put to use quickly, would keep working, and could carry the most creatures. The processes you'll learn and apply through this book (and course) meet similar goals.

For you to put these practices into use quickly, they need to support what you are already doing and to result in a net savings of time. You will learn to leverage the power of a blended model for learning and to employ techniques for peer review that allow you to follow Robyn Jackson's sage advice: "Never work harder than your students!"[3] Although designing projects aligned to standards that reinforce digital age learning skills takes hundreds of hours, fortunately this work has already been done for you. The *Who's Selling Us Now?* project is only one example of others we will explore in greater depth, taken from hundreds of others that are fully developed, ready for you to draw on and incorporate into your plans.

Once in motion, these processes must keep working. As you and your students get used to these new types of blended-model tasks, they will become self-sustaining.

Over time, the number of students whose specific needs you'll be able to meet will increase, as you learn to differentiate and select projects based on their interests as well as on areas that data tell you they need to strengthen.

We need to begin with a good road map, which means getting to the root of obstacles or problems that have prevented well-meaning educators from transforming their practice to meet the needs of digital age learners. Root-cause analysis is a problem-solving method designed to reveal the deepest (root) and most basic reasons for identified concerns. Root-cause analysis is comparable to a road map. To arrive at the correct destination, you must use the correct map. A map of Texas (no matter how good it is) will not lead anyone from Los Angeles to Santa Fe. In this section, we'll explore the tools, research, and processes designed to map your path to the goal of improved learning for all your students.

Digital Learning Project Maps: A Framework for Skill Development and Assessment

The road map for *Who's Selling Us Now?* uses a framework that is similar across subjects. Each Digital Learning Project addresses six major areas (and their subtopics) as defined by the ISTE NETS-S and is based on the Partnership for 21st Century Skills ICT maps.

Each Digital Learning Project is presented as a Project Map (examples are found in the DVD accompanying this book) that incorporates suggestions based on Robert Marzano's high-probability instructional strategies.[4] (These address the previously discussed Common Core State Standards for English, math, science, and geography.) This approach allows us to "triangulate" our strategies so that we incorporate the teaching strategies that have been found to be most effective into tasks explicitly designed to develop 21st century skills, within the context of a comprehensive view of digital age learning.

Given the natural alignment of these three leading resources, the opportunities to guide and strengthen student growth are promising. However, if we are without a means of seeing what students are thinking, these rich opportunities can slip through our fingers. Learning has often seemed like a "black box" process: we know the inputs (of time, talent, and resources), and we see, and sometimes lament, the results (in terms of student readiness for real life), but what happens inside the box—the process itself—remains a mystery.

As you learn to apply the Digital Learning Process, you and your students will gain skill in creating the evidence required to improve results, especially growth in the crucial skills that are not addressed by current methods of testing.

One of the central tenets of project-based learning is to "begin with the end in mind." Reaching our goal requires both having clear directions and a suitable vehicle. Our worthy goal, the ISTE NETS, describe the results we'd like students to be able to demonstrate after completing the learning activities we assign on a daily basis. They go far beyond "technology literacy" to address habits of mind, behaviors, and dispositions that are required to thrive in contemporary society.

All six standards are composed of four indicators that more specifically describe the skills students need to master. Every project suggests one of these four indicators for each of the six standards, as a starting point. By completing one or two projects with your entire class, both you and your students will have a clear idea of their strengths and gaps. Moreover, the process of completing additional projects as independent or collaborative group study *outside of class time* extends learning and deepens opportunities for students to develop and demonstrate mastery of the entire range of skills.

Our worthy vehicle is comprised of effective instructional strategies that we'll use to guide students to our goal. It is of critical importance that we refresh our understanding of the strategies and the context in which they are used if we are to help our students (and ourselves) arrive at mastery of the ISTE NETS.

Robert Marzano's High-Probability Instructional Strategies: Use with Care!

In the introduction to their book *Using Technology with Classroom Instruction That Works,* Howard Pitler, Elizabeth R. Hubbell, Matt Kuhn, and Kim Malenoski note:

Researchers at McREL analyzed and synthesized the results of more than 100 research reports on instruction for the past 30 years to identify categories of instructional strategies that have the most profound effect on student achievement. The analysis revealed nine categories of instructional strategies that have *a high probability* of enhancing student achievement for all students, in all subject areas at all grade levels. A report describing the findings, *A Theory Based Meta-Analysis of Research on Instruction*, was published in 1998.[5]

 All of us want to find and use the most effective strategies possible to help our students reach their highest levels of learning. Having been fortunate enough to take the Using Technology with Classroom Instruction That Works workshop, I initially paired every project activity with one of these nine strategies for enhanced achievement. It turns out I was wrong to do so, not because the strategies don't work, but because there are no "Nine Silver Bullets for Effective Strategy."

Each must be used in context, with care and thought, and our use of them in these projects has benefited greatly from Marzano's recent guidance.

Around the nation, "high-yield strategies"—classroom techniques whose utility for enhancing student achievement is supported by research—are a hot topic. However, it is essential that we develop an accurate and up-to-date understanding of these strategies. Marzano reports, "I have seen this term as the descriptor for strategies referenced in on-line courses, in district documents, and even in state documents. It is probably safe to say that I and my colleagues have unwittingly fostered this phenomenon by our comments in at least three books: *Classroom Instruction That Works* (Marzano, Pickering, & Pollock, 2001), *Classroom Management That Works* (Marzano, Pickering, & Marzano, 2003), and *Classroom Assessment and Grading That Work* (Marzano, 2006)."[6]

For example, in *Classroom Instruction That Works,* Marzano emphasized the unanswered questions about the instructional strategies he and his colleagues had identified:

- Are some instructional strategies more effective in certain subject areas?

- Are some instructional strategies more effective at certain grade levels?

- Are some instructional strategies more effective with students from different backgrounds?

- Are some instructional strategies more effective with students of different aptitudes?[7]

Marzano also cautioned that the research indicates that these instructional strategies might have a positive effect on student achievement in some situations but a negligible or even negative effect on student achievement in others. His advice: "Until we find the answers to the preceding questions, teachers should rely on their knowledge of their students, their subject matter, and their situations to identify the most appropriate instructional strategies."[8]

Marzano has recently updated his work on high-probability strategies to organize them contextually. His meta-analytical research database now describes forty-one strategies in terms of the contexts in which they are used:

- *Lesson content:* new content; practicing and deepening content that has been previously addressed; cognitively complex tasks (generating and testing hypotheses)

- *Routine activities:* communicating learning goals, tracking student progress, and celebrating success; establishing and maintaining classroom rules and procedures

- *Behaviors that are enacted on the spot as situations occur:* engaging students; recognizing adherence and lack of adherence to classroom rules and procedures; maintaining effective relationships with students; communicating high expectations

Marzano further warns, "Specifically, educators are making at least three mistakes when using the lists of strategies presented in our books (and other books like them). Left unchecked, these mistakes can impede the development of effective teaching in classrooms across the country."[9]

- Mistake 1: focusing on a narrow range of strategies
- Mistake 2: assuming that high-yield strategies must be used in every class
- Mistake 3: assuming that high-yield strategies will always work

Keeping these caveats in mind will allow us to avoid the identified pitfalls and leverage the power of research-based best instructional practices as they are integrated in an innovative blended instructional environment.

Digital Learning Use of High-Probability Strategies

Marzano's forty-one strategies for effective teaching form a comprehensive approach for all instruction, not just instruction related to the blended model we use in the Digital Learning Process. Therefore, in the descriptions of projects, I will zero in on a subset of strategies that directly help you introduce projects, dive deeper into content and processes you've previously introduced, and leverage the power of feedback to strengthen your students' learning. These strategies are embedded in the project plans themselves. A full treatment of the use of all forty-one strategies is available on Marzano's website (http://www.marzanoresearch.com/).

One area I will highlight here is the final set of strategies, which focuses on communicating high expectations. I do this in response to the unfortunate correlation between poverty, educational attainment levels, and digital access sometimes known as the digital divide. Just as in the predigital age well-meaning educators often unknowingly brought their assumptions about what students in poverty could or couldn't do (almost always underestimating their potential and depriving them of the opportunity to grow through authentic, *challenging* tasks), the high correlation between places where economic and educational attainment are weak and places where access to broadband and current technology is low can lead us to unconsciously transport this flawed thinking into the digital age. Although many (if not most) students enjoy computer and Internet access at home that is equal to or better than what they find in schools, for some students public access is their only access.

I experienced this personally when working with the most advanced students in a public high school on a pueblo in New Mexico. Internet connections did not exist outside the school and therefore ended with the school day. There were no "free Wi-Fi" coffee shops, bookstores, or other venues many of us have come to take for granted. Even cell phone coverage was dodgy. Extraordinary measures were required to remedy the situation and provide the students with alternative means of conducting their independent and collaborative online work. Although it is beyond the scope of this book to tackle the challenge of digital equity, it is essential for us to keep such equity in mind as we work with school and community leaders to implement digital learning policies.

Most of us have also become familiar with discussions of the "tyranny of low expectations" which suggests that students are held down when they suffer from our limiting beliefs about what they can accomplish. But few consider that this same dynamic may be at work for students who don't enjoy the same level of digital access as that of their more fortunate peers.

With this in mind, let's examine Marzano's strategies, which can be used in both face-to-face and online learning environments:

39. Demonstrating value and respect for low expectancy students (e.g., the teacher demonstrates the same positive affective tone with low expectancy students as with high expectancy students)

40. Asking questions of low expectancy students (e.g., the teacher asks questions of low expectancy students with the same frequency and level of difficulty as with high expectancy students)

41. Probing incorrect answers with low expectancy students (e.g., the teacher inquires into incorrect answers with low expectancy students with the same depth and rigor as with high expectancy students)

For more information about the research supporting these strategies, including how to become involved in Marzano's action research yourself, please visit http://www .marzanoresearch.com/research/researched_strategies.aspx.

Eyes on the Prize: Student Learning (Ask the Learners!)

Marzano advises, "[U]sing strategies effectively is a means to an end. The ultimate criterion for successful teaching should be student knowledge gain. Classroom strategies are tools to produce knowledge gain. Of course, this means someone must collect data on student learning."[10]

One very efficient way to gauge students' knowledge gain is simply to ask students themselves to rate how much they have learned in a given project. What may be surprising is the legitimacy of this approach. Marzano reports, "In Hattie's analysis of the research on 138 variables that encompassed 146,142 effect sizes, students' rating of their own knowledge gain had the highest average effect size. It was over three times larger than the average effect size exhibited in the 138 variables."[11] Asking students to "self-report" on their learning is an easy and apparently valid way to obtain information regarding student achievement within the context of a specific lesson or set of lessons.

Why It Works: The Research Basis for the Digital Learning Process

Root-cause analysis, mentioned earlier, seeks answers to difficult and persistent questions. One of these is why greater academic gains have not resulted from two decades and billions of dollars of investment in educational technology. The answer may be surprisingly simple: many educators do not use technology-based solutions in their everyday work because they don't feel that they need to do so to accomplish their pedagogical goals.

The types of activities that will most effectively help students learn vary with both the age and developmental levels of students, but they also vary fundamentally across the disciplines. Communication and collaboration are important for everyone, for example, but they don't help students learn to solve mathematical equations. There are key areas of each discipline that must be addressed, and not all of these are addressed by the commonalities many educational technology reformers prefer to focus on. Recent research suggests a way beyond this impasse.

Digital Learning and Technological, Pedagogical, and Content Knowledge (TPACK)

Because we tend to teach in the ways we ourselves have learned, it is essential to design for success in making the transition to a blended learning environment. Fortunately, a process for accomplishing this goal through the use of effective instructional activities has been developed by Judi Harris and Mark Hofer, based on the Technological, Pedagogical, and Content Knowledge (TPACK) model.[12] TPACK happens where teachers' knowledge of curriculum content, knowledge of general pedagogies, and knowledge of technologies intersect (see diagram).

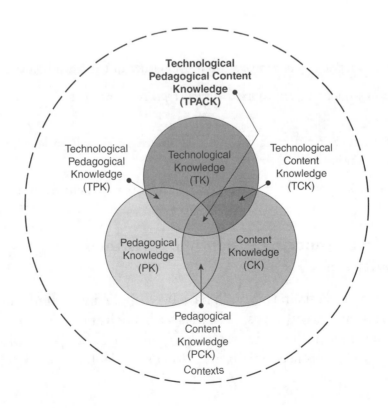

In the abstract for their paper, Harris and Hofer report, "Successful technology integration is rooted in curriculum content and students' content-related learning processes primarily, and secondarily in savvy use of educational technologies. When integrating educational technologies into instruction, teachers' planning must occur at the nexus of standards-based curriculum requirements, effective pedagogical practices, and available technologies' affordances and constraints."[13]

TPACK (appearing in the diagram's center) also comprises three particular aspects of knowledge that are represented by the other three intersections:

- *Pedagogical content knowledge:* how to teach particular content-based material

- *Technological content knowledge:* how to select and use technologies to communicate particular content knowledge

- *Technological pedagogical knowledge:* how to use particular technologies when teaching

The Digital Learning Process embeds these principles within each project, modeling effective instruction supported by digital tools and helping you design effective classroom uses of technology to support mastery of Common Core Standards. Harris and Hofer report,

[P]lanning a particular learning event can be described as the end result of five basic instructional decisions:

- Choosing *learning goals*

- Making practical *pedagogical decisions* about the nature of the learning experience

- Selecting and sequencing appropriate *activity types* to combine to form the learning experience

- Selecting formative and summative *assessment strategies* that will reveal what and how well students are learning

- Selecting *tools and resources* that will best help students to benefit from the learning experience being planned[14]

One Size Fits One: Honoring Disciplinary Distinctions Through Activity Types

The Digital Learning Projects in this book have been aligned with both the ISTE NETS-S and the TPACK learning activity types. TPACK is such a rich and deep model that this book is able to offer only an introduction; I strongly recommend that you explore it further at http://activitytypes.wmwikis.net/. Harris and Hofer's model has been developed by teams of researchers examining hundreds of activities in multiple disciplines at multiple levels; this work has revealed a surprising result: the pedagogical content knowledge is so specific to each discipline that the categories for activity types are not "hot-swappable." For example, compare the activity types for social studies and math.

Social Studies Activity Types

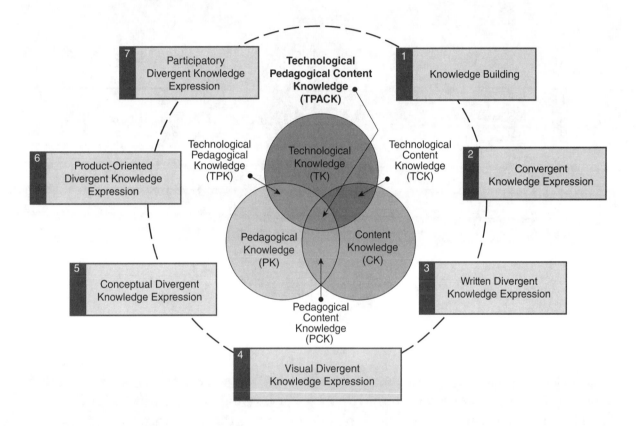

These activity types focus on Knowledge Building and Knowledge Expression, and they progress through increasing levels of student engagement.

The Knowledge Building activities in the first category are familiar: we've all been asked to read text, view presentations or images, listen to audio, participate in group discussions, and take field trips. The Product Oriented Divergent Knowledge Expression activities are a little less common student assignments: produce an artifact, build a model, design an exhibit, create a game or film. Along the way, it is critical that students come to common understandings of events, locations, and sequences (the convergent parts), as well as develop personal understandings about causes and consequences (the divergent parts). Together, these activities represent the totality of what's required to engage with the foundational knowledge, concepts, and processes that make a person fluent with the discipline of social studies.

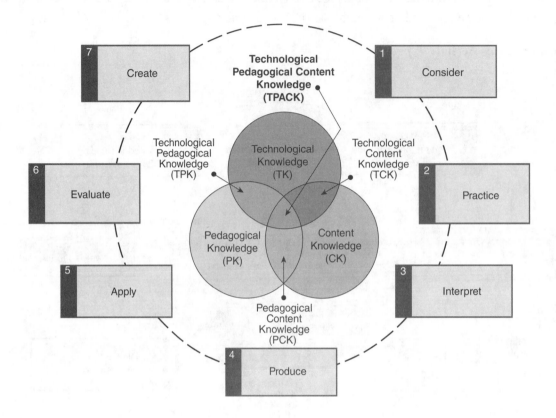

Within the Math activity types, students are asked to Consider, Practice, Interpret, Produce, Apply, Evaluate, or Create, within the context of developing mathematical skills.

Not only do the seven categories look different from those for social studies, but the contents differ too. Systematically developing mathematical reasoning involves different concepts, processes, and experiences. Instead of starting with knowledge building that leads to expression, the path asks students to recognize a pattern, investigate a concept, and understand or define a problem. Practice consists of computation or solving a puzzle. Evaluation means testing a solution, conjecture, or mathematical work.

The takeaway from this is that we will get better results from using technology if we attend to specific ways that digital tools support pedagogically sound and appropriate activities, rather than try to "fit" any specific discipline into what the technology easily does in a generic way. That's the framework I'm using throughout the Digital Learning Process, and I encourage you to explore the rich range of ideas and resources expressed in Harris and Hofer's work. As we explore the specifics of each Digital Learning Project Map, we will refer back to this organization of activities and their progression to create deeper levels of student engagement.

For further consideration, here are the specifics for science and secondary English/language arts. You may find it helpful to return to these as you begin developing the multidisciplinary projects we'll explore in later chapters.

Science Activity Types

1. Conceptual Knowledge Building Activity Types

    Read text; view presentation/demonstration; take notes; view images/objects; discuss; do a simulation; explore a topic/conduct background research; study; have an evocative experience; develop predictions, hypotheses, questions, variables; select procedures; sequence procedures; organize/classify data; analyze data; compare findings with predictions/ hypotheses; make connections between findings and science concepts/knowledge

2. Procedural Knowledge Building Activity Types

    Learn procedures; practice; prepare/clean up; generate data; collect data; compute; observe; collect samples; do procedures; record data

3. Knowledge Expression Activity Types

    Answer questions; write a report; do a presentation or demonstration; take a quiz or test; debate; develop or build a model; draw/create images; concept mapping; play a game; develop a game; create/perform

Source: *Science Learning Activity Types,* by M. R. Blanchard, J. Harris, and M. Hofer, 2009. Retrieved from College of William and Mary, School of Education, Learning Activity Types Wiki: http://activitytypes.wmwikis.net/file/view/ScienceLearningATs-Feb09.pdf.

Secondary English Language Arts

1. Reading Process Activity Types

    A. Pre-reading activity types: activating/generating prior knowledge; making predictions

    B. During-reading activity types: directed/guided reading; reading discussion; literature circles/book clubs; whole class literature study; sustained silent reading; independent reading; rereading; descriptive analysis; critical analysis/reflection; dramatic reading/reader's theater; notes; reading literature; reading nonfiction; reading other forms of text

C. Post-reading activity types: scales (surveys); summarizing; quizzing/testing; sharing/collaborating; discussion; reconstituting/reconsidering text; creating text-related artifacts

2. Writing Process Activity Types

   A. Pre-writing activity types: brainstorming/listing; doodling; webbing/clustering/semantic mapping; freewriting/guided freewriting

   B. Organizing ideas for writing activity types: sequencing/outlining/storyboarding; higher-order webbing/clustering; choosing form/genre; identifying purpose/audience

   C. During-writing activity types: drafting; conferencing; revising; editing; consulting resources; writing fiction; writing nonfiction; writing other forms of text

   D. Post-writing activity types: sharing; publishing; performing/performance

3. Language-Focused Activity Types

   A. Language exploration, awareness, and inquiry activity types: language exploration; language awareness; language inquiry

   B. Language composing activity types: sentence composing; code switching

   C. Language analysis activity types: word analysis; sentence analysis; style/error analysis; semantic analysis

   D. Language conventions activity types: mechanics; grammar; usage; language errors; spelling

   E. Vocabulary development activity types: vocabulary awareness; vocabulary analysis; vocabulary use

4. Oral Speaking/Performance Activity Types

   Speaking/speech; performance/production; evaluating/critiquing speech/performance/production

5. Listening/Watching Activity Types

   Listening actively; watching/viewing actively; multimodal/multimedia interaction

Source: *Secondary English Language Arts Learning Activity Types,* by C. A. Young, M. Hofer, and J. Harris, 2009. Retrieved from College of William and Mary, School of Education, Learning Activity Types Wiki: http://activitytypes.wmwikis.net/file/view/SecEngLangArtsLearningATs-Feb09.pdf.

Transforming Education: Insights from Chris Dede

The following material is from transcripts of a video interview with Chris Dede. He is the Timothy E. Wirth Professor in Learning Technologies at Harvard's Graduate School of Education. Dede's fundamental interest is the expanded human capabilities for knowledge creation, sharing, and mastery that emerging technologies enable. His teaching models the use of information technology to distribute and orchestrate learning across space, time, and multiple interactive media. His research spans emerging technologies for learning, infusing technology into large-scale educational improvement initiatives, policy formulation and analysis, and leadership in educational innovation. Clips from this video interview are also available on the DVD that accompanies this book.

On the Need to Aim High

Ferdi Serim: One of our very critical goals is to elevate the thought level and goals of the tasks that we are asking students to do. I know you have done so much work with simulation and enhanced learning. Is there anything you have seen that's helpful in getting teachers to have the confidence to engage students at these higher levels of thought that go beyond the traditional ways?

Chris Dede: One thing that's been characteristic of educational technology for a long time is that, when it's used well, one of the responses that everybody has (parents, school board members, teachers, professors) is we all say, "Wow, I didn't know kids this age could do that!" And yet, in fact, every time we really empower them, kids behave well above the expectations that we have, well above what we label as proficient for their age level.

So we are in sort of the Dark Ages in education, in which we constantly underestimate what kids can do. And because they are unmotivated, because the models of pedagogy are not very effective, because the content too often is watered down, then as a result the kids rise to that low level of expectation rather than going beyond.

It's so important, because part of this economic change is that the old types of industrial-era jobs are disappearing. It's very important now for all students to have 21st century skills, not just as some kind of an abstract goal, but because that is the key in the 21st century to having a decent lifestyle, a reasonable job, the chance to really engage as a global citizen. . . . What used to be good enough to get an A and a good job is now borderline, and we need to recognize that, and as advocates for kids, help them to achieve these new higher levels.

On the Connected Teaching Model

Ferdi Serim: You have touched on one other thing that I think is going to be new territory for our participants and for people in classrooms in general, and that's putting the drawbridge down over the moat that has separated the classroom life from "real life."

Chris Dede: I think informally there's a long history of individuals within the community, informal educators, community leaders, interested parents, acting as supports for teachers, but I think now we have the opportunity to move beyond that, into a connected teaching model, in which it may be that people in the community have more formal roles within the schooling system. In which schools of education start to offer different kinds of credentialing or licensing for being an informal support for teaching, as a parent, tutor, or a community member mentor, or as an informal educator guide.

This is one of the themes that, I think, will come out in the National Educational Technology Plan, which I am on the working group for. I don't know how strongly it will come out in the plan, that's still being worked through the political process, but I think it's an idea whose time has come. And just as public health now is advanced by many kinds of people, not just doctors and nurses aiding with public health, personal trainers and people in the media, and the person down the street that's lost weight and says, "You can do it too," I think that in the same way we have the opportunity with these new technologies to really help teachers by moving them into a web of partners, not just other teachers, but people throughout society.

Change Brings Both Danger and Opportunity

We are at a unique time in history: our country is facing a huge economic crisis, and when the one-time stimulus money is gone, school districts are going to be facing a situation where there is not enough money to make the old model work. So change will come, not in response to some vision so much as out of necessity. I think it's our challenge as members of the educational technology community to make sure that instead of creating simply some kind of reactive, second-best version of the old model, we instead embrace a visionary, transformative, powerful approach that uses technology to leverage doing more with less, in the way that almost every other sector of society has been able to.

As a profession, teaching is among the last segments of society to figure out how to use technology for change, and that's not surprising, because learning is a very complex human activity. But this is a turning point in history: individual teachers, small groups of teachers, and communities of practice, both face-to-face and virtual, have an enormous chance to leverage the Internet and Web 2.0 technologies for learning.

I think it's a marvelous time to be involved in this field and a chance to leave your footprints in history.

Chapter 2

Rethinking Best Practices and Digital Age Learning

Chris Dede notes, "In the next decade, schools will change more rapidly than any other societal institution. Multiple economic and technological factors are driving the evolution of 21st century educational models as different from industrial-era schools as those were from the agricultural-era one-room schoolhouse." It is projected that by 2014, 50 percent of all classes will be taught online, and standards-based, competency-driven instruction and assessments will be the norm. The meaning of effective teaching will be redefined, and new measures of teacher and school leader effectiveness will be validated and implemented at scale. Yet educators continue to be immersed in development programs that equip them for traditional careers of stand-alone, text-based instruction in self-contained classrooms.

Getting there from here will require methods that go far beyond what's been tried in the past two decades and will require comprehensive leveraging of the power of technology that has reshaped every other industry. Creating the teaching and learning environments we need in 2014 means much more than changing the delivery methods for professional development through online learning, or adding technology to traditional classrooms. It also requires changing the content, instructional methods, assessment and evaluation, and use of data as well as building effective communities of practice to allow educational professionals at all levels to collaborate in the transition to these new environments and processes.

Set against that background, our task of making Digital Learning Projects a part of your daily classroom life seems at once humble and profound. You've already been introduced to andragogy (and how the symbols will be used throughout this text). To ensure your success, it is important to use two more of the most powerful strategies available, which are introduced in this chapter: universal design for learning and project-based learning.

Creating Expert Learners: Universal Design for Learning

The goal of education in the 21st century is not simply the mastery of knowledge. It is the mastery of learning. Education should help turn novice learners into expert learners—individuals who know how to learn, who want to learn, and who, in their own highly individual ways, are well prepared for a lifetime of learning.

—Center for Applied Special Technologies

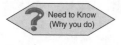 With this concise statement, the Center for Applied Special Technologies (CAST) sets out a challenge that is particularly relevant to our task. Implementing projects that harness the power of digital age learning can allow us to simultaneously create expert learners while constructing environments that support such growth in all our students.

CAST identifies three sets of characteristics shared by expert learners that are essential for us to consider as we work to strengthen creative behavior and habits of mind in our students:

1. *Strategic and goal directed.* Expert learners formulate plans for learning and devise effective strategies and tactics to optimize learning; they organize resources and tools to facilitate learning; they monitor their progress toward mastery; they recognize their own strengths and weaknesses as learners; and they abandon plans and strategies that are ineffective.

2. *Resourceful and knowledgeable.* Expert learners bring considerable prior knowledge to new learning, and they activate that prior knowledge to identify, organize, prioritize, and assimilate new information. They recognize the tools and resources that would help them find, structure, and remember new information; and they know how to transform new information into meaningful and usable knowledge.

3. *Purposeful and motivated.* Expert learners' goals are focused on mastery rather than performance; they know how to set challenging learning goals for themselves and how to sustain the effort and resilience that reaching those goals will require.

They can monitor and regulate emotional reactions that would be impediments or distractions to their successful learning.

When you take on the challenge of designing learning environments and experiences that apply these skills in authentic contexts, your path will take a significant departure from the decontextualized teaching of subject-area knowledge that forms the bulk of traditional instruction. Universal design for learning, when combined with project-based learning (described in greater detail later on), provides you with powerful strategies for creating meaningful activities.

Not surprisingly, it turns out that our brains play an important role in becoming expert learners. CAST has done incredible work in revealing how we can align our instruction to work with the natural processes our brains use to accomplish learning tasks. Because experience, environment, and heredity interact to make everyone's brain different, this means providing multiple means of

- *Representation:* presenting information and content in different ways

- *Action and expression:* differentiating the ways that students can express what they know

- *Engagement:* stimulating interest and motivation for learning

Each of these techniques supports a particular learning network in the brain.

Experience this for yourself by completing the "Your Three Brain Networks" activity at: www.cast.org/teachingeverystudent/tools/main.cfm?t_id=10.

- *Recognition networks* govern the "what" of learning (how we gather facts and categorize what we see, hear, and read). Identifying letters, words, or an author's style are recognition tasks. Multiple means of representation allow all learners to find ways to tap into their recognition networks.

- *Strategic networks* govern the "how" of learning (how we plan and perform tasks, how we organize and express our ideas). Writing an essay or solving a math problem are strategic tasks. Multiple means of action and expression allow all learners to find ways to tap into their strategic networks.

- *Affective networks* govern the "why" of learning (how learners become engaged and stay motivated, how they are challenged, excited, or interested). Multiple means of engagement allow all learners to find ways to tap into their affective networks.

Project-Based Learning: Empowering Students *and* Teachers

 Often the curriculum our students experience has not been designed to foster either creativity or critical thinking, and is delivered in a one-size-fits-all modality. Recent efforts to increase differentiated instruction are laudable, but often the adaptations are intended to increase access for students who are underperforming. It is as though we figure the gifted, creative types will do just fine on their own, which relegates considerations of fostering creativity and higher-order thinking skills to "gifted programs."

The foundational principles shared by project-based learning (PBL) and the NETS are significant and mutually reinforcing. Development of the NETS involved thousands of educators focusing on what students should know and be able to do in the digital age, as well as determining what skills and knowledge teachers require to guide such growth. The Digital Learning Process represents a convergence of these two powerful sets of ideas.

PBL has as its foundation the premise that the challenge of real-world problems can stimulate student critical thinking and sustain the high levels of engagement required to acquire and apply new knowledge. Unprepared observers entering a class where PBL is going on are confused by the activity level and the absence of a teacher standing in front of the room directing everything. In contrast, teams of students work on complex problems worthy of extended investigation. The teacher has traded roles, no longer content to merely transmit information, instead employing the skills of facilitation required to help students develop worthwhile questions, structure appropriate tasks, acquire new knowledge, and work collaboratively. Well-designed projects allow students to delve far more deeply into a subject than traditional textbook-oriented instruction permits.

 Although the task of designing and implementing PBL with a focus on digital age learning is indeed challenging, it is doable. According to Mid-continent Research for Education and Learning (McREL), "second-order change implies a fundamental or significant break with past and current practices. This type of change represents a dramatic difference in current practices. Second-order changes require new knowledge and skills for successful implementation."[1] In this chapter, we'll address the most difficult challenges in terms of design, assessment, and implementation. With this momentum, we will continue to see how Digital Learning Projects provide a pathway to the remaining NETS, both for students and teachers.

PBL and the Four D's

The Buck Institute for Education (BIE) has developed a knowledge base on PBL that incorporates the experiences of teachers who successfully use PBL in their classrooms, supported by recent research on student learning and by instructional models that incorporate authentic assessments, community-based education, service learning, internships, or career academy curriculum. BIE's highly acclaimed *PBL Starter Kit* provides in-depth insights to get people started in powerful learning strategies. To get started, visit BIE's PBL Do It Yourself page. (See BIE's website, http://www.bie.org/diy.) The project cycle comprises four essential phases: Define, Design, Do, and Debrief. Digital age communications strategies play a role in all these phases and bring different capabilities to the specific requirements of each. Let's examine the possibilities and highlight strategies you may find helpful as you build and implement your projects.

The First D: The Define Phase

"Begin with the end in mind" is sound advice, as the clarity of the goals and parameters for your project is directly proportional to its success. The five activities of this phase are (1) getting ideas for projects; (2) considering context and deciding on the scope; (3) specifying standards, skills, and goals; (4) writing a driving question; and (5) deciding on culminating products or performances (or both).

Even in the unlikely event that you can sit, Buddhalike, beneath a tree until enlightened responses to these activities arise in your mind, it is still a good idea to communicate with others as you go. Twenty-five centuries later, we have tools available to help us that the Buddha did not. *(Note: enlightenment is not an explicit goal of this book; we're just happy to guide you to the most effective PBL you've ever done!)*

1. Getting Ideas for Projects—Look Within, Look Without

Ideas for projects that connect with the real world (address the relevance factor) can come through introspection (how you honestly answer the sincere student who asks "Why on earth are we studying this?") or from reverse-engineering current events ("How did our air get this polluted in the first place, and what are we going to do about it?"). In either case, both research and feedback are called for. In the case of *Who's Selling Us Now?* the project idea came from the Partnership for 21st Century Skills. Feel free to use any of the more than one hundred projects that have already been developed as Digital Learning Project Maps, to get your feet wet.

2. Considering Context and Deciding on Scope

The *PBL Starter Kit* advises that we imagine the possibilities but know our limits, in terms of requirements, time frames, resources available in our classrooms, and knowledge levels and baseline skills of our students. As I stated previously in the description of the *Who's Selling Us Now? project,* your scope could compress into days or expand into weeks. Your academic goals determine what makes sense.

3. Specifying Standards, Skills, and Goals

In *Who's Selling Us Now?* we selected a set of English/language arts standards from the Common Core State Standards. Apart from the subject-area content standards that are addressed by your project, there are important ISTE NETS Communication and Collaboration (S2) goals embedded in every project. Students should demonstrate their ability to

- Organize ideas and develop content appropriate to audiences and situations
- Use effective oral presentation skills
- Create media that enhance content delivery
- Gauge audience reaction and understanding and adjust presentations appropriately
- Respond to questions appropriately

4. Writing a Driving Question

The *PBL Starter Kit* advises that a good driving question forms the heart of the culminating products or performances, and promotes inquiry by being motivating, open ended, or complex. A driving question should link to the core of what we want our students to learn about the subject.

Who's Selling Us Now? uses this driving question: *We are being marketed every day, but how?* The instructions ask students to choose "a variety of advertisements of products, comparing what messages advertisements are sending, which arrive, and the channels used to send these messages," and so on.

Although guiding answers may descend from mountaintops written in stone, mere mortals typically depend on communication as part of their process in developing high-quality driving questions. Information technology also allows us to see what's been revealed up on other mountaintops. Whether you are working solo or as part of a team, you'll work smarter when you can "share the brains" of people who may have already succeeded with projects similar to the one you're designing. For example, you might browse through the project descriptions found at the American Memory Project (http://memory.loc.gov /ammem/index.html), Think.com (www.think.com/en/), GlobalSchoolNet (http://www .globalschoolnet.org/gsnpr/), or ePals (http://www.epals.com). A compelling project takes its name from its driving question. See what gets you excited, and why!

Depending on your prior experience with PBL (as well as that of your students), you will find yourself somewhere on a spectrum that ranges from providing predetermined driving questions to facilitating students' developing their own (and hence taking greater responsibility for shaping the overall project design). If you are working solo, then feedback from your colleagues is invaluable. If the project idea doesn't seem clear or doable to them, it's time to go back to the drawing board. If your students will be doing the heavy lifting,

Product	Audience(s)	Technologies
Public service announcements (PSAs)	Cable TV, radio, YouTube	Digital video, animations, podcasts
Dramatizations	Community, parents	Digital video, DVDs
Documentaries (service learning)	Community, businesses, parents	Digital video, DVDs
Parent information centers	Parents	Websites, computer graphics, animations
Simulations	Students, parents, community	SecondLife, other education-oriented virtual worlds

then peer review and discussion of potential driving questions are valuable in order to keep the project real in terms of what really engages students. Discussion boards, wikis, and blogs fit this role nicely.

5. Deciding on Culminating Products or Performances

This area provides perhaps the greatest opportunities to harness the power of digital age communications, by bringing student work to a potentially global audience and allowing students to select from the full spectrum of available media.

In *Who's Selling Us Now?* I selected ninety-second video PSAs as the culminating product. Remember, increasing student engagement is the key to increased performance, and in developing your driving question, you've already made sure the project is motivating through its relevance and importance. People will care about what students produce in a situation like this, so bring on the audience! The table lists formats that make good use of digital age communications.

The Second D: The Design Phase

The BIE *PBL Starter Kit* notes that a successful plan includes the following components: a project calendar; preparing students for the project; exhibitions or culminating products and performances; developing a "grabber" that engages students; engaging in learning activities; checkpoints, assessment strategies, and rubrics; grouping of students; and obtaining the resources (equipment, facilities, technology) required for the project.

And you believed those who said, "PBL is fun, and it's easier than teaching!"? Although all this planning may make PBL appear harder than conventional teaching, the investment you make up front pays off many times as you sail by problems that you have anticipated and shift your focus to facilitating deeper, more powerful learning. Remember, most of the design work has been done for you if you make use of the Digital Learning Project Maps, so your task is more like tailoring than designing.

Either way, a key design phase decision is "Who will be in charge of the learning?" Margaret Riel is a senior researcher at the Center for Technology in Learning at SRI International. Her research focuses on the relationship between teacher learning and instructional practices mediated by technology. Over the past two decades, Riel has designed, researched, and directed Learning Circles, a program that brings student-teacher teams from different counties into PBL communities over electronic networks. Riel notes that

[An essential part of the learning process is] figuring out what it is I need to learn. We take away that process from students. We think that we can make it easier by cutting it into neat little chunks, and then all they have to do is remember this or that. But that's not learning. Learning is the planning and is the making decisions about how to organize things.

The work that teachers are doing (or the curriculum developers are doing) is really the learning. By not giving students the permission and the responsibility to be engaged in the learning process, we take away learning from them. When kids say, "School is boring," we should really sit up and listen, because learning is really exciting. If learning was really going on, it wouldn't be boring. Those two words don't go together. And so when kids say it's boring, it's because learning is not taking place in schools, and that's a really serious problem that all of us need to address.

The Third D: The Do Phase

Beginning with the very first step of a journey, you are involved with course correction. Even though every bump, obstacle, and surprise you encounter along the way presents an opportunity for learning, reaching the goal requires acting on your plans in particular ways. As identified in the BIE *PBL Starter Kit,* these components include creating a culture of inquiry; beginning the inquiry process and tasks after the "grabber" (the compelling idea you used to engage students); managing group collaboration; setting up systems to track student work; coaching the inquiry process; managing exhibitions of learning; and troubleshooting common problems.

I read all the time that technology is not a silver bullet and that wonderful projects can be done without using any 21st century tools and techniques whatsoever. Doubtless this is true, but I also wonder why anyone would choose to do so, given the wide range of alternatives. The Do phase uses technologies to end the "black box" aspect of learning, opening up windows into student performance, thinking, and problem solving.

Who's Selling Us Now? uses technology to make learning visible in several ways:

- Digital Learning Project Maps supply annotated flight plans, which you and your students constantly update.

- Discussion forums, wikis, and blogs all provide evidence of developments in student critical thinking, expression, collaboration, and problem solving.

- Final products (in this case PSAs on students becoming resilient to marketing efforts) demonstrate formative evidence of mastery as it develops throughout the project.

Helen Barrett, pioneer of e-portfolio techniques, has taught us that Evidence = Artifacts + Reflections + Validation.[2] Embedding digital age learning tools and processes within your project vastly expands opportunities to build a body of evidence that documents student learning. Inviting students, parents, and community mentors into the process goes a long way toward "walking the talk" about creating a culture of inquiry.

The Fourth D: The Debrief Phase

"Are we there yet?" and "What did we learn along the way?" are two of several questions that emerge in the Debrief phase. We have the opportunity to judge both the process (How efficient were we?) and the product (How effective were we?). The wisdom of diligence during the Define phase now becomes apparent, as both we and our students are clear as to what is expected and what constitutes success.

The BIE *PBL Starter Kit* advises that we celebrate success; facilitate student reflection about their learning; guide students in self- and group assessment; use data to plan future actions and project improvements; gather student feedback about project design and management; collect and save examples of student work; and apply lessons learned to potential future projects.

In *Who's Selling Us Now?* because the use of communication and collaboration technologies and processes were embedded within the project, at the end you will be in the happy position of having all the materials you could ever need to conduct a thorough and fruitful project evaluation. By guiding students to communicate via email, discussion boards, wikis, blogs, podcasts, and even videos, you've generated artifacts galore. By encouraging students to review and comment on one another's work, you've helped them develop and apply skills of reflection. By designing a driving question that brings authenticity and relevance to the project, you've set the stage for an audience to find meaning in your students' work.

Conclusion: Maximize Opportunities for Knowledge Building

We do well to heed Margaret Riel's words as we review the results of one project and plan for beginning the next:

Knowledge building is the purpose of teaching. It isn't getting kids to repeat what you've said. It's that they can build knowledge, not only individually, but collectively. We are in a world where people don't work alone; they work in teams. When people work, they work in settings that depend on them to be able to communicate their ideas to other people and get other people to work with them to solve problems. The problems we solve are more complex than problems that can be solved alone. We've solved the problems that are sort of simple, and we're working on ones that are really complex, and they can't be solved without working with lots of data from the past, data that we are collecting now, and lots of people who are looking at it from different perspectives with different expertise from different disciplines.

And so knowing how to do that early on is what kids need to have in school. So being involved in knowledge-building communities is a completely different way of doing school than teaching from a textbook. Take any corporation, and the people who work in that group or that corporation have different expertise. They don't just work in their own little divisions and never talk to each other. They bring their expertise to bear on a similar problem or a similar theme. In schools it would be themes and problems, and Learning Circles are problem-based; they're project-based work. And so they have themes that cut across disciplines, and that makes it possible for people from different disciplines to work together and bring their talents to the table.

Chapter 3

The Digital Learning Process

 You've seen one example of a Digital Learning Project and explored the design foundation that supports it. Now I will dive deeper into how we can structure activities so that you can observe and assess the specific skills that make up digital age learning.

Digital Learning Project Prism: Making Thinking Visible

The essential skills for student success are learning to think and learning to learn. Research in both educational theory and cognitive psychology tells us that visual learning is among the very best methods for teaching students of all ages how to think and how to learn. Visual learning techniques—graphical ways of working with ideas and presenting information—teach students to clarify their thinking and to process, organize, and prioritize new information.

The powerful combination of visual learning and technology provides four key benefits to students; they learn to

Clarify thoughts. Students see how ideas are connected and realize how information can be grouped and organized. They more thoroughly and easily understand new concepts when those concepts are linked to prior knowledge.

Organize and analyze information. Students can use diagrams and plots to display large amounts of information in ways that are easy to understand and that reveal patterns, interrelationships, and interdependencies.

Integrate new knowledge. According to research, students better remember information when it's represented and learned both visually and verbally.

Think critically. Linked verbal and visual information helps students make connections, understand relationships, and recall related details.

Using Graphical Organizers in the Digital Learning Process

The advantages of incorporating graphical organizers in the Digital Learning Process are worthy of mention here. Our goal is to make the learning visible, so that it can be assessed and strengthened. Graphical organizers today are far more sophisticated and capable than in the past, allowing for inclusion of media, links to Web resources, and collaborative authorship. They are the natural tool for the types of digital age learning you will learn to facilitate in this book.

Here is a brief summary of the types of software available:

Software	Description	License	Platform
Inspiration	Create graphic organizers and idea maps	Commercial	Mac/PC
Kidspiration	Categorize and organize ideas for writing	Commercial	Mac/PC
Cmap Tools	Construct, navigate, and share concept maps	Free	Mac/PC
Smartdraw	Draw diagrams, graphs, and concept maps	Free	PC
Concept Draw	Draw diagrams, flowcharts, and mind maps	Commercial	Mac/PC
FreeMind	Create mind mapping using Java	Free	Mac/PC
Power Point	Create concept maps using the chart feature	Commercial	Mac/PC

In the examples that follow, I use Inspiration (simply because I've been using it since 1994) to illustrate the process of having a teacher and student(s) update a Project Map. These maps allow for flexible and powerful assessment strategies. For the DVD, I've adapted these maps into interactive Adobe PDF files you can use if you don't use Inspiration. Because many interactive whiteboards now either integrate with the software listed here or provide their own utilities for creating graphical organizers, your having the ability to project these maps and have students interact in class, capture the recordings, and then access both recordings and working documents on the Web extends the possibilities almost limitlessly.

Project Maps

Each of the activities provided in the Digital Learning Process has a corresponding Project Map that is already created for you to use. As you will see, each activity is broken out into the six ISTE NETS-S, and each of these standards has its own page, where you will monitor student progress toward mastery of both the core content and 21st century skills standards. It is easier to "see" this than to describe it in text.

Here is the main activity page for the first English activity (E01).

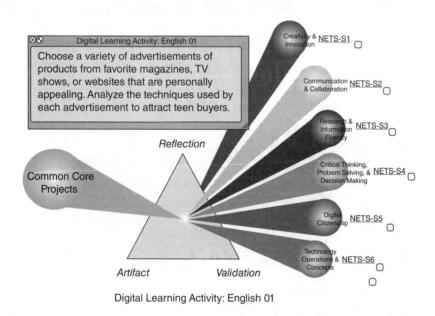

Digital Learning Activity: English 01

The upper left-hand corner contains the task description in a "note" box, so that you can always keep your "eyes on the prize." Each of the six standards on the right side of the map has a checkbox where you can indicate that a particular item will be addressed. Each standard has a circular icon, which links to a map of its own. Let's examine the Creativity and Innovation standard. In this case, the Creativity and Innovation activity seeks evidence of students' demonstrating creative thinking, constructing knowledge, and developing innovative products and processes using technology. Students: "B. create original works as a means of personal or group expression."

The rectangular boxes on the left (labeled A through D) refer to all four indicators for NETS-S1, allowing you to address the others as well. For convenience, the box directly below the ISTE NETS symbol (in this case NETS-S1) contains the project task.

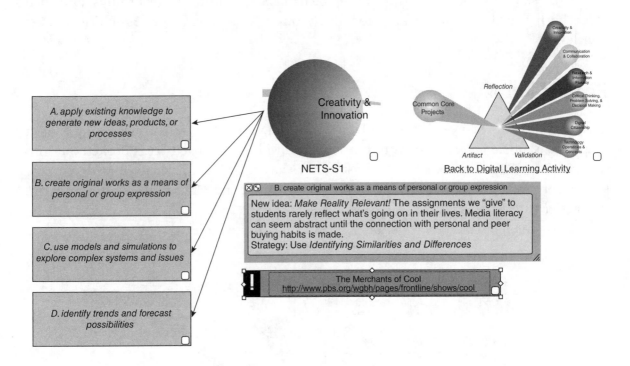

There are many ways in which students could reach this standard. They might develop and present a multimedia presentation. They might create a video podcast. They might brainstorm the form of their final product, or you might decide in advance what form their project will take.

Using the Digital Learning Trends Spreadsheet

To make the process of managing student performance data easier, I've created a spreadsheet that allows you to track student progress over time. Most likely, you already have a process you use for assigning students grades in core subject areas. This may include an electronic grade book, scores from district- and state-mandated assessments, or scores from online curriculum and learning management systems. However, keeping track of formative assessments for 21st century skills is a much less developed neighborhood. In this section, I'll introduce some of the key factors you will want to keep in mind when managing the data that can be placed at your fingertips.

The Digital Learning Trends spreadsheet allows you to accomplish four major tasks:

1. Differentiate according to need

2. Measure for growth

3. Let students take ownership

4. Watch the trends

Differentiate According to Need

Not all students are at the same level of experience or development. Using the self-assessment surveys found on the DVD as a pre- (and post-) assessment will allow your students to place themselves on a spectrum of performance and to focus on activities that will help them grow. Because 21st century skills don't fall under the mandate of "high-stakes" testing at the moment, we have additional flexibility in how we respond to student needs. The surveys ask students to rate their experience level with technology in general and the NETS-S in particular by placing themselves in one of four levels:

- 1 ≠ I've never done this

- 2 ≠ I've done this once or twice

- 3 ≠ I do this all the time

- 4 ≠ I've taught someone to do this

Using this feedback as a pre-test, you'll be able to identify and group students appropriately. Using it as a post-test, you'll be able to document growth.

The next step is to observe student progress as your classes move through the projects. Here I recommend a process I call "bird-watching." Instead of trying to find every bird in existence, many of which may not be on a migratory path past your window at this particular time of year, you use criteria to observe the birds who do happen into your view. To be more concrete (and less metaphorical), there are six ISTE NETS-S, each of which has four indicators, for a total of twenty-four standards for which we'd ultimately like students to demonstrate mastery. Not all of these will be addressed in any one project. Rather, it is important to take note of those that do. The Digital Learning Trends spreadsheet is pre-configured with places to take note of any of these twenty-four standards when student work allows you to observe the level at which students are performing.

All you need to do is use the pull-down menu to assign a score to any standard you observe being met, as follows:

4 = Goes Beyond What Was Taught

3 = Demonstrates Mastery of What Was Taught

2 = Partial Understanding, With Help

1 = Does Not Demonstrate Understanding

B8 | *fx* | PreAssessment

	A	B	C	D	E	F	G
1	NETS Summary	PreAssessment	Observation 1	Observation 2	Observation 3	Observation 4	Observation 5
2	Creativity & Innovation	1.5	2.0	2.0	2.5		
3	Communication & Collaboration	2.0	2.0	2.0	3.0		
4	Research & Information Fluency	2.0	2.0	2.0	2.5		
5	Critical Thinking, Problem Solving, & Decision Making	2.0	2.5	3.0	2.0		
6	Digital Citizenship	2.0	2.0	2.0	3.0		
7	Technology Operations & Concepts	2.0	2.0	2.0	3.0		
8	Digital Learning Activity Map	PreAssessment	E01	E01	E01		
9	Date	10/15/2010	10/18/2011	10/25/2010	11/11/2010		
10	4 Goes Beyond What Was Taught						
11	3 Demonstrates Mastery of What Was Taught						
12	2 Partial Understanding, With Help						
13	1 Does Not Demonstrate Understanding						
14							
15							
16							
17							
18							
19							
20							

NETS Summary / NETS 1 / NETS 2 / NETS 3 / NETS 4 / NETS 5 / NETS 6 / Charts

Measure for Growth

Following the advice of Robert Marzano, for formative assessments of standards-based learning we need at least five observations over time to determine the learning trends, in order to be confident that students have mastered the tasks we present. Each spreadsheet allows you to record "pre" and "post" assessment scores and then ten other observations (which could consist of five each for two projects conducted over a semester or year).

The first page of the spreadsheet shows you an overall summary of all six ISTE NETS. Subsequent pages record the detail for each standard. The final page shows you a graphical representation of the learning trends.

One important note: don't average the scores. Until you have five scores for a particular topic, you don't have enough information to make a reliable judgment, so in those cases a "?" appears as the score. Once you do have enough information, the formula in the spreadsheet calculates the correct learning trend.

Look at six. Review at least one aspect of each of the six ISTE NETS each time. Each standard has four components; it is not necessary to focus on all four at once. Review them as they support students working through the project. Ideally there should be five observations over the course of two projects. You can track two projects on the spreadsheet between pre and post observations as it is presently set up.

For example, in this case we're looking at Creativity and Innovation (NETS-S1).

The pre-assessment shows that this student completely didn't understand use of models and simulations, and was similarly at a loss about identifying trends and forecasting possibilities. Therefore, the first two observations led the teacher to focus on helping the student gain understanding of these concepts in order to use them in the project.

See if it sticks. Look for consecutive validation of observations.

- Any trouble area gets evaluated in the next cycle, until the next level is reached.

- Moving up from one level to the next gets revalidated in the next cycle, and then every other cycle until it is validated a total of three times.

Let Students Take Ownership

Peer review with teacher validation is the strategy I recommend. As noted previously, Marzano has found that once students understand the standards they are trying to meet, their self-assessment is as reliable as any externally developed standardized test. Let's harness this potential. As teachers, we only need to focus on the 1's (students who have no clue and really need our help) and the 4's (students whose work goes beyond what we've taught and is so superior that it deserves wider recognition). Students themselves can assign 2's and 3's, and when their "self-nomination" for having displayed mastery is subject to peer review, self-policing is often more stringent than teacher grading.

	A	B	C	D	E
1	**Creativity & Innovation**	PreAssessment	Observation 1	Observation 2	Observation 3
2	Students demonstrate creative thinking, construct knowledge, and develop innovative products and processes using technology. Students:	1.5	2.0	2.0	2.5
3	A. apply existing knowledge to generate new ideas, products, or processes.	2.0	2.0		2.0
4	B. create original works as a means of personal or group expression.	2.0	2.0		3.0
5	C. use models and simulations to explore complex systems and issues.	1.0	2.0	2.0	
6	D. identify trends and forecast possibilities.	1.0	2.0	2.0	
7					
8	Digital Learning Activity Map	PreAssessment	E01	E01	E01
9	Date	10/15/2010	10/18/2011	10/25/2010	11/11/2010
10					
11	4 Goes Beyond What Was Taught				
12	3 Demonstrates Mastery of What Was Taught				
13	2 Partial Understanding, With Help				
14	1 Does Not Demonstrate Understanding				
15					

Here are some guidelines to use:

- Peer review happens every cycle, with immediate teacher validation of all 1's and 4's and periodic review of each student's portfolio for levels 2 and 3.

- Students generate questions to initiate moving from level 1 to level 2. Example: "You mean it's OK if I don't already know what I'll find out or why it happens before I set up my experiment?"

- Student feedback that results in another student's moving up a level is rewarded, when the student providing the assistance is identified and the progress is verified.

- Peer review validates that all level 3 artifacts are appropriately ranked. Any level 3 artifact should be suitable for "spot platforming" as an example of high-quality work.

- Level 4 is rare. Any level 4 work, once verified, is platformed at the "hall of fame" level on internal and external websites.

Watch the Trends: Data Review and Analysis

Use both the NETS summary matrix (shown earlier) and the charts to identify successes and challenges.

The summary matrix allows you to see at a glance where to focus your efforts (in this case, Creativity and Innovation presented an early challenge for this student) and when to introduce "next steps" based on student readiness. In the case illustrated, focusing on 4B (planning and managing activities) allowed progress in Critical Thinking, Problem Solving, and Decision Making to set the foundation for subsequent improvement in several related NETS areas.

The progress chart view provides another way to keep track of what's working and what areas need more support. (Note: the chart will appear "flatlined" until you've made an assessment and entered data. The y axis shows the performance level students have reached [higher is better], and the x axis shows their progress over time.)

Guiding Growth, Generating Evidence

The Digital Learning Process is both formative (showing progress along the way) and summative (showing that students reached the goal). It responds to the challenges of capturing mastery of skills that are particularly hard to assess (such as "positive attitude" or "demonstrating personal responsibility for lifelong learning").

Helen Barrett, a pioneer of e-portfolios, has elegantly described the requirements for evidence of learning. These consist of having artifacts to examine, which then provide material for reflections. The artifacts can be evaluated according to criteria provided by rubrics and then validated for the degree to which they meet a set of standards. This is the schema we use in the Digital Learning Process.

Artifacts

The Project Maps provide a means to organize student work from three sources. Students can

- Enter descriptions of the activities they perform directly into text fields

- Insert hyperlinks to external Web resources (websites, blogs, wikis) they're using

- Attach files to the Project Map file (any type of document they create)

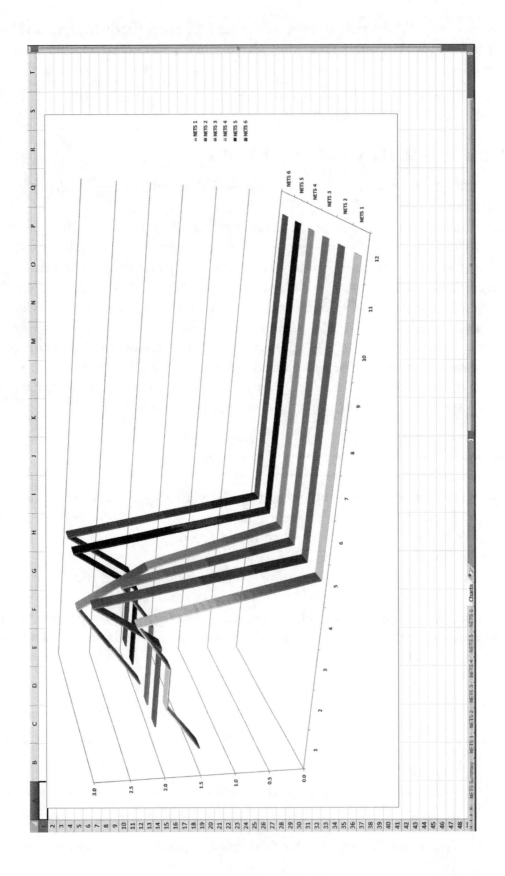

Any of these artifacts can be commented on by students, teachers, or peers as required; the following figure shows a student contribution. The artifacts grow through participation, as the conversation continues and deepens over time.

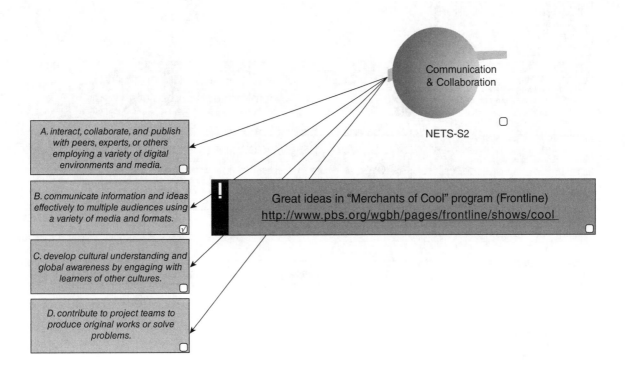

Reflections

Reflections are an important (and sometimes the only!) way to observe student learning, especially for higher-order thinking and problem-solving skills. Students can choose from the entire spectrum of communications technologies available at your school (multimedia, digital audio and video, website creation, wikis, blogs, and so on). In this case, the teacher is asking the student about ideas that came from watching the show, and how they will be used with the team (forcing thought about collaboration).

Evaluation

Asking students for specific information addressed in project rubrics, backed up by data and sources, allows for a level of evaluation that is difficult to accomplish in traditional reports, whether they are paper based or PowerPoints.

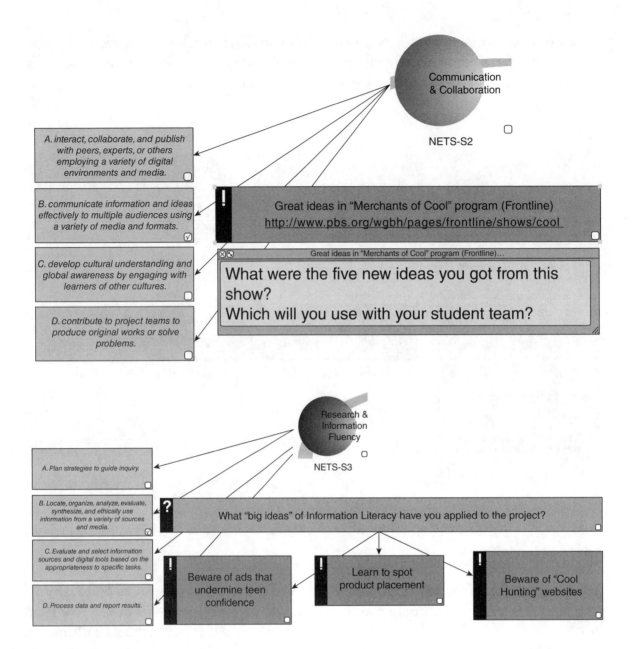

Validation

In the case of English Activity 1, developing media literacy is the prime objective. Traditionally, we might list goals such as these:

The project task addresses a high-priority need and requires the learner to:

- *Determine the information basis* of the problem to be solved

- *Reformulate* a complete statement of the task

- *Understand and follow directions* presented in a variety of media (printed, spoken, electronic)

Within the Project Map, we can color-code any student responses (questions in the green boxes from the teacher) according to rubric level, where

Blue = top ranking, as in Blue Ribbon

Green = meets the standard, as in "good to go"

Yellow = caution, as in "needs more work"

Red = "stop, look, listen" and begin again

(See the color version of this diagram on the DVD.)

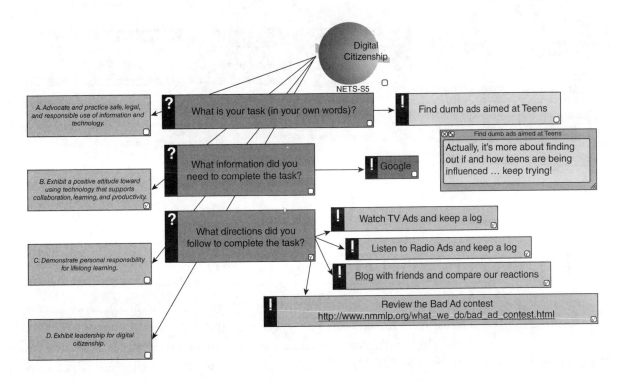

Providing Guidance

Project Maps are a "work in progress," so they are ideally suited to provide feedback as projects are developed and completed. The Digital Learning Project Maps were built using symbols for each of the ISTE NETS-S, so you don't need to add them in. However, you have complete flexibility about adding any other objects that are necessary.

For example, if students are focusing on Research and Information Fluency and they are tasked to discover the most reliable and accurate sources for information about teen advertising, they can add objects for each of their sources.

The beauty of digital documents (PDFs or Inspiration) is that these objects can contain URLs (links to websites) that are "live" in the document. If a student finds a website like the New Mexico Media Literacy Project and includes the link in the object (as shown here), when you go to review the student's Project Map, one simple click will take you to the website.

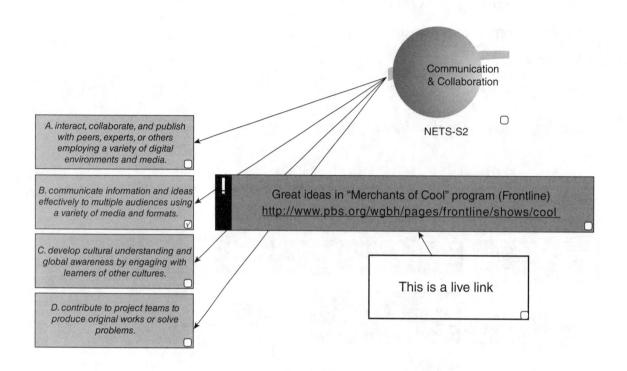

The "Look Fors" of Digital Age Learning

The power of the Digital Learning Process is that the projects are already developed. This section gives you a "behind the scenes" view to understand the principles that shape each project's design, so that you can know how to assess each of the ISTE NETS. Let's begin with one of the toughest: Creativity.

Assessing Creativity: Learning What to Look For

Through discussion forums, journals, presentations, and more traditional written products, students are providing us a window into their thinking processes. Students' writings will show us when they've begun to look at objects and ideas from many different points of view. Students must learn to use knowledge, skills, and appropriate strategies to generate ideas, select among alternatives, and persevere in their efforts. Once you become aware of what to look for, evidence of creative efforts becomes easier to see and to build on. The following are some examples, adapted from *Intel Education's K–12 Teaching Tools* Assessment Tools for Thinking (Creativity):[1]

Developing original and inventive ideas. Students enjoy playing with ideas and thinking of new things to do and make. Students make existing objects, ideas, processes, and systems more efficient, beautiful, or ethical. For example, students may generate ways to improve everyday objects.

Patterns and comparisons. Students create metaphors and analogies from unlike objects and ideas that provide new insights and understanding, often in areas very different from their primary area of expertise (for example, sports and art, jokes and mathematics, machines and music). Students see unusual patterns and notice how objects and ideas are alike and different in the world around them, in concrete and abstract environments.

Humor. Students appreciate and employ many kinds of humor, such as irony, wit, sarcasm, and parody.

Language. Students use language in meaningful, novel ways. Students *use* the tools of writing and speaking to create powerful images and strong arguments to persuade, inform, and entertain. They *appreciate* the subtleties and intricacies of powerful and beautiful language. Students successfully manipulate the *conventions* of language, such as spelling, grammar, literature, storytelling, and speaking, to enhance meaning.

Application of content knowledge. Students use an in-depth knowledge of a subject area and its tools to create objects, ideas, systems, and processes that are unusual or have never been seen before.

Idea generation and synergy. Students think of numerous new ideas with or without specific guidelines. Students enjoy working with others because hearing others' ideas and bouncing their own ideas off others helps in generating more ideas.

Strategic flexibility. Given a specific goal, students can come up with several subgoals and a variety of ways to achieve them.

Risk-Taking and Creativity

If we knew what it was we were doing, it would not be
called research, would it?
—Albert Einstein

There is a delicate and important balance between risk-taking and success in creative endeavors. Here are elements to look for in student responses (adapted from *Intel Education's K–12 Teaching Tools* Assessment Tools for Thinking [Creativity]), which you can use to guide your project development:

Is open to novelty. Students enjoy trying new ideas and processes.

Evaluates consequences. Students weigh potential benefits against possible negative consequences when deciding to take a risk.

Adopts a healthy approach to mistakes. Students' concern about making mistakes does not prevent trying a new process or idea. Students admit mistakes when they happen, and analyze experiences to learn from mistakes.

Perseveres. Students believe that success in new activities depends on hard work, preparation, and being careful.

Is self-confident. Students follow their own path and do not give in to peer pressure on important subjects, even after considering peers' opinions.

Judgment and Creativity

 It is also crucial that students develop the skills of discernment they need to guide their progress on a path of continuous personal improvement. Valuable indicators for these behaviors include observing when

- Students determine whether *ideas are worth pursuing*.

- Students *add details necessary* for implementing and improving ideas.

- Students independently and reasonably *evaluate the quality* of products and performances.

- Students show *confidence in the quality of work* based on knowledge of the relevant content.

Rejecting the Tyranny of *Or* for the Genius of *And*: The Power of a Blended Model

 The blended model combines the best elements of face-to-face and online learning to produce a result neither could achieve separately.

John Hattie recently reported the results of one of the most comprehensive syntheses of research ever conducted on factors that have an impact on student achievement. "Hattie's synthesis considered over 800 meta-analyses and 52,000 research studies. At the conclusion of his analysis, Hattie advised that the best way to improve schools is to have teachers work in collaborative teams to clarify what students should learn, gather evidence of that learning through ongoing formative assessment processes, and use that evidence to inform and improve their practice."[2]

It is quiet enough here in Santa Fe to faintly hear skeptics around the country shouting "and exactly when will we find the time to do that?!?" Clearly, the face-to-face model, which requires substitutes, travel costs, and a host of other logistical nightmares, makes such a strategy far-fetched in a time of budget reductions. But what if no one had to go anywhere? What if these collaborative teams could log on to a computer and see student work, check formative assessment data, and discuss modifications to practice from anywhere, at any time?

Similar objections are raised to adding PBL to existing curricula for students. All of the existing time in the school calendar and curriculum maps is spoken for, and in too many schools, mandated assessments and the test prep that comes with them are edging out time for science and social studies, let alone the arts, service learning, and anything else "not on the test."

One possible answer is to migrate a substantial part of both student and teacher learning to the online environment, and reserve a bit of precious face-to-face time for periodic management of these processes. The Digital Learning Process is designed to provide an on-ramp for introducing this blended model to your learning organization (or "school," as we used to call it back in the 20th century).

The blended model avoids the isolation and lack of immediacy that often result when online programs are built by merely posting face-to-face curriculum on a website. A blended model also makes possible several powerful strategies that don't scale in a completely face-to-face environment:

1. Organizing people into a system of cascading mentorship (whereby you are simultaneously a protégé of someone more advanced and the mentor for someone who's trying to learn something you recently mastered), through statements like these:

   • Here's what I need to learn and why.

   • Here's how I'll be using it, and what I aim to gain.

   • Here's the instructional context where I'll apply what I learn.

   • These are the roles that I've played, that I am good at, and that I am willing to play here.

   • This is the role I want to prepare to play next:

     • Lead others through this course, after completion

     • Coach a site-based study group

     • Coach an online study group

2. Allowing all of the above for students (in case you didn't think of that)

3. Allowing competency-based (rather than "seat time"–based) professional development

4. Allowing competency-based (rather than "seat time"–based) student achievement

5. Allowing coaching and mentorship from screened and approved Science, Technology, Engineering and Mathematics (STEM) professionals or other 21st century professionals in your community

Collaborative Online Learning: Insights from Margaret Riel

 *During the filming of the Digital Learning online course, Margaret Riel gave a series of insightful interviews, and her specific advice appears here. The five elements of leadership for online collaborative learning she discusses are based on her thirty years of work and research in building online communities, PBL, and school transformation. Please keep these in mind and return to them as you implement the Digital Learning Process in your classroom, school, and professional learning networks. Whether you see yourself as a leader right now or not, Margaret's vision of leading from any seat makes these observations something you "need to know." Clips from this video interview are also available on the DVD that accompanies this book.*

> I think the important thing is that anybody can lead from any seat, that is, a leader is somebody who inspires others to be better. We talk a lot about service leadership, so that the leader isn't the person who runs up ahead and says, "This way! We're all going this way!" The leader is the person who manages to inspire the other people to follow them. And that means that they have a message, they have something that other people enjoy, and are inspired by listening to.
>
> —Margaret Riel

1. People Need to Learn from Practice on a Regular Basis

The first premise of leadership, in my way of thinking about it, is that people need to learn from practice. They need to learn every day, and *they need to have a systematic process for learning from practice*. It isn't just kind of, "I am going to do this and think about it a little bit." It means that they are going to pick specific things that they do each time or each term and say, "I am going to learn from this, I am going to collect some data, I am going to reflect on this. I am going to think about if this is the best way to do this, or if it's reaching the people and having the effect in the classroom that I expected to have." And so the first thing in leadership in my mind is to be someone who learns from practice on a regular basis.

2. You Need to Help Students (and Others) Become More Powerful in What They Do Every Day

The second thing is, once you have a procedure, kind of an action research frame of mind, for learning, then how do you interact with other people? You need to have a strategy for how you are going to work with other people so that they don't feel like you are discounting their value, because they bring important information to the setting. Making them better is really in my mind what leadership is about, it's not about taking what I do and getting other people to copy me, it's about making somebody else better. In our Pepperdine program, we talked about *our role is to make our students more powerful versions of themselves; that's our charge.* How do we through action research help the students to become more powerful in what they do every day?

3. Lead Through Your Social Networks—Diffusion Is Across Networks

The third level is that not only do you need to lead locally but in order to really have the benefit of your social networks, *you need to reach beyond the people that you are locally working with;* that means professional organizations, that means networking, because that's where the new knowledge comes from. You can gain some amount of knowledge within your own contacts, but you need to be able to reach out to what's going on beyond because good ideas spread in diffusion across networks. So that's the next level, really cementing those relationships, those professional organizations, and your role in them.

4. You Can't Really Teach Anyone You Don't Have a Relationship With

We find that you can't really teach anyone you don't have a relationship with, and that relationship is really a critical part of teaching. I don't think we emphasize that enough: students who say "My teacher doesn't even know my name" will not listen to that teacher in the same way they will to a teacher who says, "Megan, I am so glad to see you this morning," or "How was the soccer game?" *Those things that we think are not really critical to the content are really critical to the learning,* and you know I just can't say how important it is for those people who teach to really develop this relationship with the people that they are working with.

5. Reaching Across Time Is Important Too—Leave Your Ideas in a Form Others Can Interact With

Reaching across distance is important, but also reaching across time is important, and the way you reach across time is you leave conceptual artifacts. Now I could say you write articles or publish papers, but in this wonderful world that we're in right now, you've got all sorts of media that you can use to create productions, to create conceptual artifacts. But *leaving your ideas in a form that other people can interact with over time as well as across distance* is a really important part of leadership.

Unfortunately, in education, teachers mostly retire without leaving a single conceptual artifact for the next group of teachers to learn from, and that's why teachers' teaching is taking so long for us to develop as an art and science, because the practitioners are not the people who are building the knowledge base; the researchers are building the knowledge base, but they don't have the grounded knowledge the teachers have.

So I see the technology in two ways: both what can be done with it in the classroom—and I think that's what most people focus on—but it's also a terrific tool for including teachers in a learning environment, which I think is missing in schools and in a leadership environment; both of those two are critical.

Chapter 4

Do Try This at Home!
Checking Your Digital Age Teaching and Learning Tool Kit

The future is already here—it's just not very evenly distributed.
—William Gibson

Unlike the digital natives we teach, most of us took varied paths to develop our existing digital skills. Those of us who began early (pre-Internet) had a particularly torturous path and have witnessed a continual and accelerating ease of use and increase of power in the numbers and types of technologies learners have at hand. However, even the youngest entrants to the profession, who grew up in a networked world, have trouble translating the dazzling array of tools into effective practice. The truth is that you can't master anything you've not been exposed to, so it is important to *take a look* at what's commonly available now, *take stock* of how these capabilities extend the learning experiences you provide, and *take charge* of your strategy for keeping your tool kit current.

In this chapter, we will review four classes of tools that are essential for digital learning:

- Anytime and real-time communication and collaboration tools

- Content creation tools

- Data management tools

- Google Earth, GPS, and GIS tools

We explore these topics at a high level because focusing on contextual purpose has a longer shelf-life than any set of ever-evolving tools. For "up-to-the-minute" information about any of these tools and the practices they support, we highly recommend exploring two online resources: Classroom 2.0 and Kathy Schrock's Guide. The Digital Learning website and DVD have links to both, as well as to all the tools described in this chapter.

Anytime and Real-Time Communication and Collaboration Tools

One of my favorite sources for information on everything is Kathy Schrock. This preference goes back nearly two decades, when Kathy began collecting the best Internet education sites and resources in a file box. She has an unmatched ability to track emerging technology trends and discern the essential from the distracting. Kathy has provided her own compendium, which you access at http://KathySchrock.net. The site provides a dynamic list of Web 2.0 resources using a tool called Diigo that she continually updates for aggregators, blogs, and feeds from different sources. She includes collaboration tools; graphic organizers, such as Bubbl.Us; ways of sharing files, such as drop.io; and online applications, many of which are free, so that you don't have to pay and you don't have to download.

Kathy Schrock's Web 2.0 Tools

http://www.diigo.com/list/kathyschrock/web20tools

Sometimes the people you want to work with are online when you are, and sometimes they aren't. Your digital learning tool kit needs to support your strategies for both situations. One great place to go to learn about either is Classroom 2.0 (http://classroom20.com), which is on a social network called Ning, which connects you to an entire community that brings its questions and resources there. Classroom 2.0 also supports a wiki, which is a compendium of information provided by the community. The categories are quite extensive: blogging, calendars, cell phones, Google Earth—everything you could possibly think of that you might want to do—and this is a resource that is added to and maintained by the membership. It is also organized by subject, by grade level, and by other categories as well. Classroom 2.0 does require registering for a free membership, which is well worth the time.

Sometimes it is good to have a tutorial, and among the things that Classroom 2.0 provides are links to excellent videos by Lee Lefever of Common Craft. One of the most widely shared is "RSS Feeds in Plain English," which is posted on YouTube. Because in many cases YouTube is blocked by schools, there's another version of this service called TeacherTube, which also contains versions of the *In Plain English* series of tutorials and is more often accessible from schools.

Anytime Communication Tools

Anytime tools allow you to make information publicly available that can be seen and responded to at the convenience of the viewer. One analog equivalent would be the bulletin board outside a grocery store, restaurant, or place of work. Frequently the bulletin board information would contain a way for people to contact each other in real time (by providing a phone number); today there are multiple strategies for taking the conversation further.

The following videos are available on TeacherTube. You will need to register for a free account to access them, but this is a good idea, as TeacherTube is often one of the few video sites not blocked in schools.

"Blogs in Plain English"

http://www.teachertube.com/members/viewVideo.php?video_id=12423

"Wikis in Plain English"

http://www.teachertube.com/members/viewVideo.php?video_id=6538

"Google Docs in Plain English"

http://www.teachertube.com/members/viewVideo.php?video_id=9618

Real-Time Communication Tools

Sometimes the nature of your communication or collaboration needs demands that you shift into immediate contact. Over the years, many of us have adopted the rule of "three emails, then a phone call" because the missing subtleties in tone and inflection and the potential for misreading intent that come with the territory of email seem to multiply when several are sent in a matter of minutes. Now we don't even need to use the phone, thanks to Voice over Internet Protocol (VoIP) and free videoconferencing options. The following collections of videos and materials are available on Classroom 2.0:

"Skype: Using Videoconferencing to Enhance Learning"

http://live.classroom20.com/1/category/skype/1.html

"Guide to Using Elluminate"

http://live.classroom20.com/using-elluminate.html

"Instant Messaging"

http://wiki.classroom20.com/Instant+Messaging

"The Case for Instant Messaging in the Classroom"

http://www.speedofcreativity.org/2006/08/28/the-case-for-instant-messaging-in-the-classroom/

Live editing

    Etherpad (http://etherpad.com/)

    Google Docs (http://vodpod.com/watch/497154-google-docs-in-plain-english)

Voice/video collaboration

    Skype (www.skype.com)

    Elluminate (www.elluminate.com)

    Adobe Acrobat (www.acrobat.com)

Content Creation Tools

A fundamental precept of digital learning is to move students from being consumers to producers of content. Further, this creation process can now be collaborative. Professionals have had sophisticated tools for decades to make movies, music, and books, but now the capabilities of these tools have migrated to "the cloud" (software that runs on Internet servers, not on your local computer). Google Docs is a great example of this movement, and a great place to begin your explorations. The second link organizes tools by learner types, a very useful approach for educators.

    Google Docs explained

    http://vodpod.com/watch/497154-google-docs-in-plain-english

    "100 Web Tools for Every Kind of Learner"

    http://www.collegeathome.com/blog/2008/06/10/100-helpful-web-tools-for-every-kind-of-learner/

Data Management Tools

Data management is often overlooked, for several reasons. First, the term *data* now has accountability baggage, as its most common use is as part of a "gotcha" strategy. Second, data management is usually somebody else's job, as its back-office past as a highly technical function meant that one needed to be a programmer in order to operate technically sophisticated software. Considering that many educators consider spreadsheets to be advanced technology applications, databases seem a distant and irrelevant category of tool. However, if our challenge is to understand and respond to the needs of each student, to differentiate instruction for our students, and to keep track of what's worked best for whom, then making friends with technologies that can help us seems very reasonable. Luckily, the applications themselves have recently become more friendly and are freely available on the Internet. Zoho Creator is a good example (http://www.zoho.com/creator/index.html).

It is also advisable to check with your district IT leaders to confirm what may already be available to you via site license. For example, many districts who have site licenses for Microsoft Office have the ability to provide Access database software, but it is rarely requested by teachers. You won't know until you ask!

Google Earth, GPS, and GIS Tools

Paradoxically, the power of digital learning technologies to "liberate learning from locality" simultaneously makes "place-based learning" more vibrant and relevant than ever. The former concept means that students are no longer limited by resources (experts, information, tools) that are not nearby. Students in rural New Mexico can have the same access to remote sensing devices, including telescopes, electron microscopes, and space probes, that students living down the block from the world's finest research facilities enjoy. What was unforeseen until recently was the power that geographic information system (GIS) tools add to the learning equation. Databases of imagery and environmental, demographic, political, economic, and historical data now can be blended in ways never before considered. It is exciting to watch the body of our professional knowledge grow on a daily basis; you can confirm this for yourself by visiting the resources listed here:

Google Earth

http://earth.google.com/

The place to get started, download software, and explore. Google Earth lets you fly anywhere on Earth to view satellite imagery, maps, terrain, and 3-D buildings, from galaxies in outer space to the canyons of the ocean. You can explore rich geographical content, save your toured places, and share with others.

Google Earth Blog

http://www.gearthblog.com/index.html

Contains great project ideas and links to resources.

Chapter 5

Eyes on the Prize!

If the prize is student learning, there are conflicting places to look. If the prize is student learning *that prepares students for expanded options in the digital age,* we may even have to look outside of school. If we're following Margaret Riel's first element of leadership *(people need to learn from practice on a regular basis),* then nobody made you look, because you are always looking, both at how your students are doing and how you can improve your practice to serve them better.

This chapter offers you examples from each discipline of what to look for in terms of student mastery of digital age learning skills, embedded in the context of projects based on academic standards. In *Who's Selling Us Now?* you saw an overview of one project's map. The examples here are selected from the more than one hundred project maps that have been created in four core content areas (English/language arts, mathematics, science, and social studies/geography).

Creativity and Innovation (NETS-S1)

Creativity is the trickiest element to assess, and carries cultural baggage about how (or if) it can actually be taught.

In using project-based learning (PBL) to reach the first of the ISTE NETS-S, Creativity and Innovation, we must begin by moving beyond widespread misconceptions about creativity and refresh our information with what's been learned from the study of the creative process and creative people. As it turns out, our work is integral to the health and vibrancy of creativity within our culture, not just in our classrooms. The choices we make about how we structure the activities that take place in classrooms, particularly the authenticity and relevance of the challenges we ask our students to engage with, can either nurture or extinguish creativity in our students.

Students demonstrate creative thinking, construct knowledge, and develop innovative products and processes using technology. Students:

A. apply existing knowledge to generate new ideas, products, or processes.

B. create original works as a means of personal or group expression.

C. use models and simulations to explore complex systems and issues.

D. identify trends and forecast possibilities.

Creativity: A Closer Look

It is significant that the first NETS for both teachers *and* students challenges us to "go beyond" what is in the textbook; to generate new ideas, products, or processes; and to create original works. Upon inspection, we may discover unexpected conceptual baggage regarding creativity, who is creative, and how we can strengthen these behaviors and habits of mind in our students and ourselves.

In his book *Creativity*, Mihaly Csikszentmihalyi suggests that "creativity is a process by which a symbolic domain in the culture is changed."[1] Creativity results from the interaction of a system composed of three elements: a culture or domain that contains symbolic rules, a person who brings novelty into this symbolic domain, and a field of experts who recognize and validate the innovation. More important, "creativity does not happen inside people's heads, but in the interaction between a person's thoughts and a sociocultural context."[2] The implications for digital age learning are huge, as it provides the context for the required intersection of the person (our students), the domain (subject-area knowledge), and the field (people who work with the content in "real life").

What's most important to us is Csikszentmihalyi's observation, "It is easier to enhance creativity by changing conditions in the environment than by trying to make people think more creatively."[3] He adds, "If too few opportunities for curiosity are available, if too many obstacles are placed in the way of risk and exploration, the motivation to engage in creative behavior is easily extinguished."[4] Let's explore how digital age learning can serve as an effective lever in transforming the environment in ways that nurture and strengthen creativity in our students, as we help them become expert learners.

Creativity 101 for Educators

For many people, "creativity" means "gifted"; and traditionally, serving the needs of such students is beyond the charge of general classrooms. CAST's introduction of "creating expert learners" as a goal does much to remedy this problem. Because the problem is that the term *creativity* as commonly used covers too much ground, Csikszentmihalyi distinguishes three different usages of this term. In our work with PBL, we'll need to address the needs of all three, and even go beyond them, if we are to reach our goal of helping all students become expert learners.

The first usage *(brilliant)* refers to people who express unusual thoughts, who are interesting and stimulating—in short, people who appear to be unusually bright. Brilliant people would be those identified for Gifted and Talented programs through psychometric testing and access to IDEA funding, for example. Even in Lake Woebegone (where everyone is above average), brilliant people would be rare. Can you think of someone from your high school yearbook who'd have been "most likely to be tagged brilliant"?

The second usage *(personally creative)* refers to people who experience the world in novel and unusual ways. These are individuals whose perceptions are fresh, whose judgments are insightful, and who may make important discoveries that only they know about. Personally creative people form a minority of the general population; they often don't care that they may seem "different" from the mainstream, and indeed celebrate their difference. Can you think of someone from your high school yearbook who'd have been "most likely to be tagged personally creative"?

The final use *(creative types with a capital C)* designates individuals who have changed our culture in some important respect. You probably can't think of anyone from your high school yearbook in this category, because this type of accomplishment is rarely achieved before adulthood (but you might find him or her on Wikipedia!).

Designing for Creativity: Learning Where to Look

Helen Barrett teaches us that Evidence = Artifacts + Reflections + Validation,[5] so let's examine what each of these elements could consist of as we design projects that are intended to provide evidence of reaching NETS-S1: Creativity and Innovation.

Note that for purposes of introducing the interaction between Common Core State Standards and the NETS, examples of all four NETS-S1 (Creativity and Innovation) indicators will be provided in this discussion. For the remaining five NETS, similarly detailed explorations will be found on the DVD and not in the text of this book.

What Does NETS-S1 (Creativity and Innovation) Challenge Students to Do in English?

In the 21st century, literacy takes on an expanded definition, one in which everyone must function as reader, author, editor, researcher, publisher, and information professional at one time or another. Communications can take on more forms than ever before, and students must become fluent in each one. Moreover, the comprehension and synthesis aspects of locating, interacting with, and applying information in all forms are entry-level expectations of 21st century employers.

Students demonstrate creative thinking, construct knowledge, and develop innovative products and processes using technology. Students:

A. apply existing knowledge to generate new ideas, products, or processes.

Creators and Innovators—Endangered Species? Don't creativity and innovation require freedom? Doesn't information "want to be free"? How do people make a living "being creative" if their work can be copied and distributed without compensation? Who "owns" intellectual property, anyway (authors, publishers, customers)? Create a multimedia presentation that illustrates the most common violations of the rules governing intellectual property, trademark, copyright, fair use, and plagiarism, and present responsible alternatives for each violation.

B. create original works as a means of personal or group expression.

Whose Words Are They, Anyway? If you didn't write them, find out! If someone used yours, find out! Create a multimedia presentation that illustrates responsible research practices that students can use to avoid plagiarism. Develop several versions of your presentation (print, Web, multimedia) that deliberately include inappropriate copying of material that is not properly credited. Have team members track down the violations and report back how they detected the offenses.

Learning Strategies

Use Cooperative Learning to provide students with opportunities to interact with each other in groups in ways that enhance their learning.

C. use models and simulations to explore complex systems and issues.

On Your Mark! Get Set! Know! Design a process to determine the speed and quality of information as it reaches you from different media. The stopwatch starts the moment you learn of an event. From that point, compare when it shows up: online, in print, on broadcast TV, on cable TV, and on radio. Also track the level of detail in initial reports and those that follow.

D. identify trends and forecast possibilities.

Reality, Reading, Experience? Ways of knowing evolve with our changing abilities to investigate, conceptualize, and communicate. In the novel *The Last Book in the Universe*, by Rodman Philbrick, the main character poses the question, "Why bother to read any more if you can just *probe* [experience the world exclusively through virtual "reality"]?" Participate in a panel discussion, giving a reaction to this question from one of these viewpoints: William

Shakespeare, a Sony executive in charge of the PlayStation division, a science fiction author, a student of 1990, a student of 2050.

Learning
Strategies

Use Cooperative Learning to provide students with opportunities to interact with each other in groups in ways that enhance their learning. By taking on roles representing different points in history, students can gain new perspectives on what we know, how we know, and how we transmit knowledge.

What Does NETS-S1 (Creativity and Innovation) Challenge Students to Do in Math?

Students demonstrate creative thinking, construct knowledge, and develop innovative products and processes using technology. Students:

A. apply existing knowledge to generate new ideas, products, or processes.

Fool's Gold? Discover what techniques are effective at twisting facts to fit a purpose, and how to recognize when you're being fooled. Explore the Web page "How to Lie with Statistics" at http://staff.washington.edu/chudler/stat3.html. Find examples of graphs and other data representations from the media to assess their truthfulness and ability to persuade or mislead a reader. (Math Strands: data analysis, probability)

B. create original works as a means of personal or group expression.

Water Is Life! Although we take fresh water for granted, shortages are predicted to become a crisis on a global scale in the coming decades. Creative and innovative solutions will be required. First, people need to become aware of the magnitude of the problem and how our daily habits have a global impact. Use visual representations to compare current global water use and available resources. Join the Down the Drain project at http://www.k12science.org/curriculum/drainproj.

Learning Strategies

Use linked tables, graphs, and symbolic representations (as can be displayed in a spreadsheet) to explain how components of a real-world situation are connected and how changes could impact worldwide water use. (Math Strands: data analysis, probability)

Use Nonlinguistic Representation to enhance students' ability to represent and elaborate on knowledge using mental images. Data from the Down the Drain project and other online databases can be used to generate graphics and animations that show comparative uses of water on local, regional, national, and international bases.

C. use models and simulations to explore complex systems and issues.

Same Problems, Different Answers? People everywhere have similar basic needs (food, shelter, clothing, education). Yet local circumstances determine which solutions are workable and which are not. Ask students to formulate questions related to their physical environment and how similar needs are met in two contrasting populations or cultures, by designing studies that can answer the questions, collecting appropriate data, and presenting conclusions. (Math Strands: numbers and operations, data analysis)

Learning Strategies

Use Identifying Similarities and Differences to enhance students' understanding of and ability to use knowledge by engaging them in mental processes that involve identifying ways that items are alike and different.

D. identify trends and forecast possibilities.

Model the Future! Growth patterns are the result of complex interactions. Some patterns are linear (for each family, you need one more house or apartment); some are algebraic (the children in each family are usually different ages and will go to different schools), and the ratio of families with young children to retirees will create a different balance of needs for social services. Project changes in the physical size of your community over the next fifty years based on population trends, using physical and digital models to demonstrate the underlying mathematical concepts. (Math Strands: numbers and operations, algebra, geometry)

Learning Strategies

Use Identifying Similarities and Differences to enhance students' understanding of and ability to use knowledge by engaging them in mental processes that involve identifying ways that the forces shaping growth patterns are alike and different.

On *Model the Future*

The following material is from transcripts of a video interview with David Thornburg. Clips from this video interview are also available on the DVD that accompanies this book.

Well, I think it's a wonderful challenge, because to start with, any time you are dealing with the community, you are dealing with the student's own life, so it has a personal connection.

The amount of labor that it takes to look at census data for their community, identify population distributions, which involves, among other things, graphing data, etc., it's very, very rich. And then the question is, when you start forecasting the future from all of this, there are new things that have to be added to it. For example, mortality rates in the community; how does the population-age cohort shift throughout time?

I mean, we have seen, for example, in the United States, we had the baby boom and then the baby bust, and then the echo boom, over a long, long period of time. Any time you are talking about fifty years or so, which is the subject of this particular challenge, you have got two generations to deal with.

So you not only have to take a look at the people who live today, but you also have to take a look at the people who are being born, which means looking at birthrates, and then the likelihood of them having children in the future.

Now this is where it starts to get tricky, because people who are already born, you can take statistics, and given how health care operates and longevity increases over time, because of medical advances, you can make fairly accurate estimations of what that population cohort is going to look like in the future. That's how insurance companies work; they understand how to do this very well. And going a generation out, that's easy to do too, because we know the birthrate today of children, etc.

What we don't know, though, is what that next generation is going to be like. I mean, for example, if there is radical global climate change, maybe the population density of a particular area is going to change. Maybe it's going to change, not because of climate change, it's going to change because people just found another cool place that they want to live and move to. We saw that in California during the boom years, when a lot of people in the hi-tech industries were leaving and going to places like Utah and Oregon and other places, where small towns were suddenly getting very large because of these migrants from other states.

So this type of problem is wonderful; it involves a lot of creativity and speculation, but it is also grounded in a nice quantitative set of data, and it's quite possible, and highly likely in fact, that two different students using the same data sets will come up with different projections for the future; not perhaps radically different projections, but different projections just the same.

And this is important, because in mathematics, a lot of people feel that mathematical problems all have that—if you have one problem, there is one answer to that problem. And the fact is a lot of mathematics is a tool to help you formulate multiple answers to a problem.

What Does NETS-S1 (Creativity and Innovation) Challenge Students to Do in Science?

Students demonstrate creative thinking, construct knowledge, and develop innovative products and processes using technology. Students:

A. apply existing knowledge to generate new ideas, products, or processes.

Science—It's Everywhere! Beyond the obvious links to science, technology, engineering, and math (STEM) careers, science skills show up in all sixteen Career Clusters. Career Clusters provide a tool for seamless transition from education to career in this era of changing workplace demands. They categorize any possible employment into one of sixteen categories that allow people to define a pathway into those careers. (See http://www .careerclusters.org/ for more information.) The sixteen clusters are shown in the figure.

Using a variety of information resources, ask students to create a personal presentation that explains which science-related Career Cluster is their most and least favorite, in terms of providing attractive possibilities and direction for life after high school. (Science Strand: science in personal and social perspectives)

B. create original works as a means of personal or group expression.

Living Room! What would happen if your home started to shrink or be divided so that you couldn't get from one part to another? If you could ask an animal or plant, it would be able to tell you: this is what habitat loss and fragmentation are all about. Ask students to explain the effects on plants and animals of the loss of their natural habitat, using a wide range of tools and a variety of oral, written, and graphic formats (for example, diagrams, flow charts, simulations, graphs) to share information and results of observations and investigations. (Science Strand: Earth and space science)

Learning Strategies Use Nonlinguistic Representation to enhance students' ability to represent and elaborate on knowledge using mental images. Create an animated map that shows projected changes in population, housing, schools, businesses, and other factors identified through student research.

C. use models and simulations to explore complex systems and issues.

Recycling—Hope or Hype? Recycling efforts have gained popularity across the nation, providing a simple and visible contribution that individuals can make to conserve energy and natural resources. Ask students to create a model that shows whether local efforts are producing the desired results. Students should investigate whether local recycling efforts help conserve energy and natural resources, using a broad range of tools and techniques to plan and conduct an inquiry to address the question. (Science Strand: Science in personal and social perspectives)

Use Identifying Similarities and Differences to enhance students' understanding of and ability to use knowledge by engaging them in mental processes that involve identifying ways that use of energy and natural resources for recycled and nonrecycled materials are alike and different.

D. identify trends and forecast possibilities.

Plan Ahead! Some new schools are overcrowded the first day they open. This happens when school building can't keep pace with new housing. Build a model to help the community know how many new schools it will need when new housing developments are planned. Identify factors to be considered in making informed decisions about land use and in deciding whether a new housing development will require building additional schools and, if necessary, where new schools should be built. (Science Strand: Science in personal and social perspectives)

Use Identifying Similarities and Differences to enhance students' understanding of and ability to use knowledge by engaging them in mental processes that involve identifying ways that factors related to land use decisions are alike and different.

What Does NETS-S1 (Creativity and Innovation) Challenge Students to Do in Geography?

Students demonstrate creative thinking, construct knowledge, and develop innovative products and processes using technology. Students:

A. apply existing knowledge to generate new ideas, products, or processes.

Do You Hear What I Hear? Music defines teenage identity as much as clothing. But how does the music that students in your school listen to compare with what the rest of the nation is listening to? How much of this music is purchased, downloaded, heard by broadcast, or shared? Ask students to use the Internet to locate and download data about teenage purchases of recorded music, then collect local data from students about their music purchases and prepare graphs comparing this data for a multimedia presentation to the class.

Learning Strategies
Use Cues, Questions, and Advance Organizers to enhance students' ability to retrieve, use, and organize what they already know about music styles and student listening and purchasing habits.

B. create original works as a means of personal or group expression.

From Debate to Drama! Economic and environmental facts can seem abstract and distant. These factors become personal immediately when people's livelihood and way of life are at stake. An effective drama creates believable characters on both sides of the issue, bringing to life the situations where these factors clash. Ask students to write a dialogue and storyboard a video for two people expressing different points of view on the same geographic issue, such as a foreman of a logging crew and a conservationist debating the use of a national forest.

Learning Strategies
Use Identifying Similarities and Differences to enhance students' understanding of and ability to use knowledge by engaging them in mental processes that involve identifying ways that perceptions about the health and purpose of forests are alike and different, between people on both sides of a geographic issue.

C. use models and simulations to explore complex systems and issues.

Be Prepared! Challenge students to determine the risks posed by possible natural disasters by examining how local geographic features and human constructions shape the possible responses to each type of event. Students should develop a community response plan in the event of a natural disaster, working collaboratively on a team using a geographic information system (GIS) to develop models. Each community has volunteer or professional first responders, as well as public safety staff. Students can work in teams to gather information from these people and to research existing emergency response plans from communities facing similar risks.

Learning Strategies
Use Cues, Questions, and Advance Organizers to enhance students' ability to retrieve, use, and organize what they already know about the possible consequences of local natural disasters.

D. identify trends and forecast possibilities.

Livable Cities? What environmental quality challenges are shared by large cities around the world? How do local conditions determine which possible solutions are workable for each city? Ask students to develop innovative plans, including specific recommendations illustrated by maps, to improve the quality of environments in large cities around the world, weighing the benefits and drawbacks of each plan.

Learning Strategies

Use Identifying Similarities and Differences to enhance students' understanding of and ability to use knowledge by engaging them in mental processes that involve identifying ways that environmental quality issues in different cities are alike and different.

Assessing Creativity and Innovation (NETS-S1)

Knowing where to look and what to look for is crucial for teasing out evidence of student growth in Creativity and Innovation. Rich artifact sources include personal journals, discussion forums, emails to teachers and coaches, postings on wikis, and blogs.

The Intel Teach Assessment library contains rubrics on a wide array of topics, which is available for free (after you register) at http://educate.intel.com/en/AssessingProjects. Here are several categories I've gathered from that site for you to consider, as well as statements describing highly desired student behaviors:

Developing original and inventive ideas

- Students express that they enjoy playing with ideas and thinking of new things to do and make.

- Students discuss their efforts to make existing objects, ideas, processes, and systems more efficient, beautiful, or ethical.

Patterns and comparisons

- Students' writing includes metaphors and analogies using unlike objects and ideas that provide new insights and understanding, often in areas very different from their primary area of expertise (for example, sports and art, jokes and mathematics, machines and music).

- Students describe unusual patterns and notice how objects and ideas are alike and different in the world around them, in concrete and abstract environments.

Humor

- Students' writing includes appreciation and use of many kinds of humor, such as irony, wit, sarcasm, and parody.

Language

- Students use language in meaningful, novel ways. Students use the tools of writing and speaking to create powerful images and strong arguments to persuade, inform, and entertain.

- Students appreciate the subtleties and intricacies of powerful and beautiful language. They successfully manipulate the conventions of language, such as spelling, grammar, literature, storytelling, and speaking, to enhance meaning.

Application of content knowledge

- Students use an in-depth knowledge of a subject area and its tools to create objects, ideas, systems, and processes that are unusual or have never been seen before.

Idea generation and synergy

- Students' writing includes thinking of numerous new ideas with or without specific guidelines.

- Students' writing indicates that they enjoy working with others because hearing others' ideas and bouncing their own ideas off others help in generating more ideas.

Communication and Collaboration (NETS-S2)

Need to Know (Why You Do)

Communication can take on more forms than ever before, and students must become fluent in each one. Moreover, the comprehension and creative aspects of locating, interacting with, and applying information in all forms are entry-level expectations of 21st century employers.

Communication may be the defining element of our digital age, as technology brings new meaning to "anywhere, anytime" and increasingly makes us all "connected." I remember seeing a *National Geographic* article in 1960 about the electrification of Appalachia, in which a farmer explained why he turned down the opportunity to have a telephone, saying, "I don't like the idea of having a bell in my house that anyone in the world can ring." Today, people must seek out those rare and remote destinations where their cell phones and wireless modems can't be reached in order to savor a few days or hours of solitude and restoration.

Yet when we embark on the path of enhancing learning through digital learning and of empowering these projects with the full range of means and methods available to us in the digital age, whether to connect or not is not an option, as communication is the gatekeeper for success (as in "do not pass Go, do not collect $200").

Students use digital media and environments to communicate and work collaboratively, including at a distance, to support individual learning and contribute to the learning of others. Students:

A. interact, collaborate, and publish with peers, experts, or others employing a variety of digital environments and media.

B. communicate information and ideas effectively to multiple audiences using a variety of media and formats.

C. develop cultural understanding and global awareness by engaging with learners of other cultures.

D. contribute to project teams to produce original works or solve problems.

What Does NETS-S2 (Communication and Collaboration) Challenge Students to Do in English?

Students use digital media and environments to communicate and work collaboratively, including at a distance, to support individual learning and contribute to the learning of others. Students:

A. interact, collaborate, and publish with peers, experts, or others employing a variety of digital environments and media.

Project task: Search information from a variety of print, online, and nonprint sources for a report on a topic of personal interest related to the Holocaust. Evaluate the information using criteria for validity and reliability. Discuss your findings with peers online, providing your rationale for any sources suspected to be unreliable.

New idea: *Share Our Brains!* Use blogs to collect preliminary information and share reflections on emerging patterns of validity and bias. Compile peer-reviewed examples on a wiki.

College and Career Readiness Anchor Standards for Writing

Production and Distribution of Writing – Grade 8

- Use technology, including the Internet, to produce and publish writing and to interact and collaborate with others.

Learning Strategies

Use Cooperative Learning to provide students with opportunities to interact with each other in groups in ways that enhance their learning. Invite experts encountered through research to review and comment, using the wikis and blogs students have created.

B. communicate information and ideas effectively to multiple audiences using a variety of media and formats.

Project task: Given a variety of hyperlinked documents on a topic of personal interest, describe your own process for reading and evaluating a website or other text containing a variety of embedded links, share these reflections online, and compare processes with classmates.

New idea: *Web 2.0 to Gather, Organize, and Share!* The "read-write" Web provides a perfect environment for transforming individual efforts into group products.

Learning
Strategies

Use Cooperative Learning to provide students with opportunities to interact with each other in groups in ways that enhance their learning. By capturing and comparing individual strategies used to evaluate links (included in both print and online materials), reflections allow best practices to emerge.

C. develop cultural understanding and global awareness by engaging with learners of other cultures.

Project task: Collaborate with email pals and online mentors from other cultures and geographical areas in order to write a collaborative essay or create an interactive, interpretive project. Partner up with classes from other cultures through the free projects provided by ePals (http://www.epals.com), once you've registered for a free account, which is required to access the projects.

New idea: *Beyond Boundaries!* Our mental images of people and places often form before we've had any personal interactions or information as a basis. Capture the "before" and "after" versions of the cultures, landscapes, and daily life of your students' global partners for later comparison.

Use Nonlinguistic Representation to enhance students' ability to represent and elaborate on knowledge using mental images.

D. contribute to project teams to produce original works or solve problems.

Project task: Create a class survey on the various communication methods class members have used outside school in the last month; identify and explain observed patterns.

New idea: *Walk the Talk!* Use a range of technologies to gather the information. This can include Web-based surveys, email, text messages, and print and phone.

College and Career Readiness Anchor Standards for Writing

Production and Distribution of Writing – Grade 8

- Use technology, including the Internet, to produce and publish writing and to interact and collaborate with others.

Use Cooperative Learning to provide students with opportunities for interacting with each other in groups in ways that enhance their learning. The result will be to collaboratively create a class survey on the various communication methods class members have used outside school in the last month.

What Does NETS·S2 (Communication and Collaboration) Challenge Students to Do in Math?

Students use digital media and environments to communicate and work collaboratively, including at a distance, to support individual learning and contribute to the learning of others. Students:

A. interact, collaborate, and publish with peers, experts, or others employing a variety of digital environments and media.

Project task: Measure and compare the amount of time spent in school and at home doing homework, watching TV, playing video games, and communicating with friends (using cell phones, the Internet, and so on). Create graphical representations of data using graphing calculators, spreadsheets, and other data visualization tools.

New idea: *A Portrait in Multitasking!* A tally of how many hours students spend on different tasks will often total more than twenty-four hours a day, because so many activities happen at once.

Learning Strategies

Use Nonlinguistic Representation to enhance students' ability to represent and elaborate on knowledge using mental images. Tables of numbers alone can't portray the reality of how students use time as well as the mediums of video or animation can.

B. communicate information and ideas effectively to multiple audiences using a variety of media and formats.

Project task: Read the Web page "How to Lie with Statistics" at http://staff.washington.edu /chudler/stat3.html. Find examples of graphs and other data representations from the media to assess their truthfulness and ability to persuade or mislead a reader.

New idea: *Try It Yourself!* Use the techniques presented in the "How to Lie with Statistics" Web page to make dubious statements about various aspects of school life (for example, surveys or grades) and ask students to distinguish graphs and other data representations that are correct from those that are flawed.

Use Nonlinguistic Representation to enhance students' ability to represent and elaborate on knowledge using mental images. Direct students to collaborate with classmates to create a set of

Learning Strategies

valid and invalid graphs, charts, and other visual representations of data for evaluation by students, parents, and teachers.

C. develop cultural understanding and global awareness by engaging with learners of other cultures.

Project task: Students formulate questions related to their physical environment and how similar needs are met in two contrasting populations or cultures, by designing studies that can answer the questions, collecting appropriate data, and presenting conclusions.

New idea: *What Works and Why?* Have students find partners in other locations or cultures to compare and analyze how similar needs are met and how these solutions reflect the local physical environment.

Learning Strategies

Use Summarizing and Note Taking to enhance students' ability to synthesize information and organize it in a way that captures the main ideas and supporting details about how each culture or population meets similar needs.

D. contribute to project teams to produce original works or solve problems.

Project task: Prepare a budget to fully equip a student rock band, DJ, or sports team, by using e-commerce to obtain estimated costs (such as for items available on eBay).

New idea: *Canvass the Community!* You never know who has exactly what you need in their attic or garage.

Learning Strategies

Use Cooperative Learning to provide students with opportunities to interact with each other in groups in ways that enhance their learning. Investigate what is available locally, either for donation or for a low price. Fill in the gaps with online research.

> ## Common Core State Standards
>
> ### Mathematical Practices (Grade 8)
>
> 1. Make sense of problems and persevere in solving them.
> 2. Reason abstractly and quantitatively.
> 3. Construct viable arguments and critique the reasoning of others.
> 4. Model with mathematics.

> ## Common Core State Standards
>
> ### Mathematical Practices (Grade 8)
>
> 5. Use appropriate tools strategically.
> 6. Attend to precision.

What Does NETS-S2 (Communication and Collaboration) Challenge Students to Do in Science?

Students use digital media and environments to communicate and work collaboratively, including at a distance, to support individual learning and contribute to the learning of others. Students:

A. interact, collaborate, and publish with peers, experts, or others employing a variety of digital environments and media.

Project task: Investigate the possible relationships between variations in weather, performance of school sports teams, and moods of students, by executing the steps of scientific inquiry. (Science Strand: science as inquiry)

New idea: *Tell the Story with Data!* Understanding the relationships between three separate variables (weather, scores, and moods) is a complex task. Visual representations of data can be more effective in highlighting these relationships.

Use Nonlinguistic Representation to enhance students' ability to represent and elaborate on knowledge using mental images. Use spreadsheets or other data visualization tools to communicate findings.

Learning
Strategies

B. communicate information and ideas effectively to multiple audiences using a variety of media and formats.

Project task: Develop a chronological model or time scale of major events in the formation of the earth, using a wide range of tools and a variety of oral, written, and graphic formats (for example, diagrams, flow charts, simulations, graphs) to share information and results of observations and investigations. (Science Strand: Earth and space science)

New idea: *Too Big for Words!* Given that most people live only a century or less, time scales of billions of years quickly become too large to understand. Visual representations can portray such huge relationships in ways not possible with words alone. Collaborate with peers and experts to develop a chronological model or time scale of major events in the formation of the earth, using a wide range of tools and a variety of oral, written, and graphic formats (for example, diagrams, flow charts, simulations, graphs) to share information and results of observations and investigations.

Use Nonlinguistic Representation to enhance students' ability to represent and elaborate on knowledge using mental images.

Learning
Strategies

C. develop cultural understanding and global awareness by engaging with learners of other cultures.

Project task: Participate in simulation or role-playing activities to examine the ethics of the complex issue of stem cell research. Compare and contrast information found in a variety of websites, blogs, and wikis with regard to authenticity and voice, then prepare to take on roles representing either opposing view. (Science Strand: science in personal and social perspectives)

New idea: *The Power of Place!* Collaborate to gather information from a wide variety of sources and cultures, and determine how local values and beliefs shape positions on the issues.

Use Summarizing and Note Taking to enhance students' ability to synthesize information and organize it in a way that captures the main ideas and supporting details.

Learning
Strategies

D. contribute to project teams to produce original works or solve problems.

Project task: Collaborate with a network of learners to investigate the societal, ecological, and political issues surrounding the availability of drinkable water, using a variety of digital collaboration tools. (Science Strand: science in personal and social perspectives)

New idea: *Pool Information Resources!* In the United States, people take water for granted, whereas in other communities, people must carry water every day for miles, from the nearest well to their homes. This task keeps many children from attending school. Find global partners and ask about their situations. Collaborate with a network of learners to investigate the issues surrounding the availability of drinkable water, using a variety of digital collaboration tools (phone, video, synchronous and asynchronous virtual classroom platforms).

Learning
Strategies

Use Cooperative Learning to provide students with opportunities to interact with each other in groups in ways that enhance their learning.

What Does NETS-S2 (Communication and Collaboration) Challenge Students to Do in Geography?

Students use digital media and environments to communicate and work collaboratively, including at a distance, to support individual learning and contribute to the learning of others. Students:

 A. interact, collaborate, and publish with peers, experts, or others employing a variety of digital environments and media.

 Project task: Collaborate with peers to create a series of Web pages that use maps to portray information about your hometown (for example, a community atlas).

 New idea: *Map Your Community!* Select the most interesting and relevant features of your hometown and then use Google Maps or Google Earth to generate images to create a community atlas. Organize into groups that focus on particular aspects of hometown life (sports, entertainment, dining, and so on).

> ## Geography Activity Types: Convergent Knowledge Expression, Visual Divergent Knowledge Expression
>
> Students use pictures, symbols, and/or graphics to highlight key features in creating an illustrated map.

Learning Strategies

 Use Cooperative Learning to provide students with opportunities to interact with each other in groups in ways that enhance their learning, by focusing on their community.

 B. communicate information and ideas effectively to multiple audiences using a variety of media and formats.

 Project task: Have students create original data sets of locations in the community that they select, using tools such as a global positioning system; input spatial data into spreadsheets; and present their findings using variety of media.

 New idea: *Nominate Local Landmarks!* What places would students show a visitor from a different country? Organize teams that will research their candidate landmark and make their case for inclusion in the final presentation.

> ## Geography Activity Type: Knowledge Building
>
> Students extract and/or synthesize information from maps, charts, and/or tables.

Learning Strategies

 Use Cooperative Learning to provide students with opportunities to interact with each other in groups in ways that enhance their learning, by focusing on their community.

C. develop cultural understanding and global awareness by engaging with learners of other cultures.

Project task: Use the Internet to locate and download data about teenage purchases of recorded music, then collect local data from students about their music purchases; prepare graphs comparing this data for a multimedia presentation to the class.

New idea: *Jam with Global Partners!* There are several ongoing global projects and groups (such as GlobalSchoolNet [http://www.globalschoolnet.org], YouthCaN [http://www .youthcanworld.org/], and ePals [http://www.epals.com/]) that can help in connecting students around the world to determine what music teenagers in different parts of the world listen to and purchase.

Use Cooperative Learning to provide students with opportunities to interact with each other in groups in ways that enhance their learning. Organize teams that focus on particular regions or nations to gather information from distant peers.

Geography Activity Types: Convergent Knowledge Expression, Visual Divergent Knowledge Expression

Students use pictures, symbols, and/or graphics to highlight key features in creating an illustrated map.

Learning Strategies

D. contribute to project teams to produce original works or solve problems.

Project task: Work on a team to write and create a video about immigrants to a new country struggling to deal with the issues involved in adapting to an unfamiliar environment.

New idea: *Use Universal Language!* Create a video that could work with or without a sound track, by virtue of common situations and gestures that are used in everyday life. Record two versions of the sound track, one in English and one in the language of the immigrants who are the subject of the video.

Geography Activity Type: Visual Divergent Knowledge Expression

Students use pictures, symbols, and/or graphics to highlight key concepts in creating a dramatic video.

Learning Strategies

Use Nonlinguistic Representation to enhance students' ability to represent and elaborate on knowledge using mental images.

It's hard to understand the benefits of technology until they are seen in the context of helping you accomplish the most vital tasks you face. Technology will not (and should not) replace traditional modes of communication. But just as you wouldn't want to walk everywhere, neither would you want to fly. In contemporary society, anyone who does not know how, when, and when not to use a particular method of communicating is increasingly communication handicapped.

Communications, Then and Now

Communications in the analog age were periodic (the daily newspaper, the nightly news, the monthly PTA newsletter, the constant PA interruptions); their formality or casual nature was understood in terms of the container that delivered them. (The personal note was handwritten; the draft board notice was typed.) Communications today are all over the map! Anyone and everyone can be an author, changing the basis of *authority* and increasing demands on consumers to validate the quality of the information they consume.

Many of us straddle these ages, having learned in a time when Ozzie and Harriet could be seen on black-and-white TV, but teaching in classrooms where students have seen the same shows on Nick at Nite. In analog age classrooms, the teacher stood at the front of the room and used a chalkboard to display words and drawings, while students took notes

Aspect	Analog Age	Digital Age
Audience	Fixed by venue	Boundless
Directionality	One-to-one, one-to-many	Omnidirectional
Authority	Earned	Optional
Frequency	Periodic, sequential	Constant, simultaneous
Formality	Defined by contents	Defined by channel

from lectures (sometimes passing notes between themselves if they could avoid being caught) until the bell rang and they moved to another similar classroom at the end of forty-five or fifty minutes. The words that were studied were written by people whose academic achievement conferred sufficient authority for those words to be printed in books, which were then published in large quantities and used in classrooms across the nation.

Can you guess which generation finds that classroom a bad fit? That's the point of this section: we can leverage the power that's available to us now, power that has never before been used to improve learning in a systematic way.

Communications Dimensions, in General

Communications vary in terms of when they happen (right now or anytime?), where they happen (right here or anywhere?), how we're engaged (participant or spectator?), and how we learn about them (do we reach out for them, or are they thrust upon us?). Knowing your purpose determines when to use any particular method. In the "old days," communications consisted of spoken (or sung) words, written words, and images. Thomas Edison and his peers added recorded sound (spoken and nonverbal) and moving images to the mix. These "big 5" modalities still comprise the content of our communications. What has changed is how they can be shared, who can see them, how they can be interacted with, and how they can be used together to build new knowledge on a massively distributed scale.

A decade ago, these dimensions had boundaries that were more defined, but with Web 2.0 (aka "the read-write Web"), it seems that soon almost any content will flow through almost any channel.[6]

Keeping Pace with Emerging Technologies

One of the most useful Web-based resources for staying current with the field of emerging technologies for learning is EDUCAUSE's "7 Things You Should Know About . . ." (http://www.educause.edu/ELI7Things?bhcp=1). In the EDUCAUSE Learning Initiative's (ELI's) ELI Jan-Feb08 poll, participants identified *critical thinking* as the most important skill we can teach our students to prepare them for Life 2.0. When asked "What types of activities or learning environments will foster critical thinking in the classroom?" the three leading responses were

- Complex problem solving (scenarios with ill-defined problems and open to many interpretations)
- Authentic learning or "learning by doing"
- Case-based learning

Team collaboration also topped the list of important skills for Life 2.0. When asked "What technology offers the most promise for creating meaningful team collaboration?" the three leading responses were

- Wikis
- Collaborative document editing (for example, Google docs, SubEthaEdit)
- Discussion boards

In the following sections, we'll explore the specific role communications skills play in the success of your projects, and strategies that leverage the power available to you and your students.

Paula White, Apple Distinguished Educator and gifted resource teacher in Albemarle County, Virginia, explains how adding a wiki to the way her class "does business" has shifted the culture of learning, setting a good foundation for online collaborative work.

I created an educational wikispace. With that, the kids get email, which you can "close" to be only open to the members of your wikispace. (Internet safety has to be a major concern to deal with, so not only is it closed to the general public's comments/editing, but I also have parent permissions signed!) I invited them all to be members (including parents, so they could observe) and then they began emailing.

The funny thing is that there were at least four out of eleven initial members on our wikispace WORKING over spring break. (I can't tell who "lurks" without logging into each account, so there may have been more watching.) They created two book pages and began several web pages on topics of their interests. One kid wrote us all while she was waiting in the airport on her way to Florida, complaining about not getting there until 2 AM. <grin> I know those of you who travel to present can relate to THAT frustration! That email became part of the impetus to have a "spring break 08" page where they were sharing what they were doing while away from each other!

The typical email I get from kids (usually at night, at home) is something to the tune of "Hey, Ms. White, can I create a web page that will show how our fundraising for the fifth grade present to the school is going?" Or, "Will you invite me to join the logical thinking page so I can work on it?" or "Can I begin our Ghost Cadet page over break?" (He did, and set up a nice hierarchy that the rest of the kids gave him great feedback on when we got back.) They are clearly aware of their possible audience—one kid who decided to do a page on "teachers' different teaching styles" said she couldn't write some of what she thought because the person might read it and she didn't want to hurt her feelings. She worked really hard to name the things she enjoys and appreciates about this teacher.

At home, at night, on the weekends, they are asking me to be able to do "educational" tasks . . . They write, edit, share, ask for advice, email, and most importantly of all, I think, feel part of a learning community.

I have to say the best question I've heard thus far, though, is "Will we still be able to keep doing this kind of work over the summer?"

The important factors here are that students are provided a protected environment in which what they write can be seen by those who need to see it, and commented upon by peers, parents, and mentors as required. Students take ownership of such spaces, and the more they post, the more artifacts there are for reflection. Using rubrics, peer editing can improve products, and final validation by you can guide students to mastery of the goals you designed at the outset of your project. No more "flying blind"!

Communication and Collaboration with High-Probability Strategies

Digital age communication and collaboration potentials are daunting in their scope, especially for those of us who would not self-identify as "digital natives." Your success in focusing these potentials in order to derive the maximum benefit for learning is increased by using the right strategies. The inspiring, creative part is how you bring Marzano's high-probability strategies into your project. One way is to systematically ensure that you use at least one of these strategies as the basis for each email or online direction you provide. Examples follow:

Context	Content	Strategy
Email	Wow, I saw online that you worked late on revising the storyboard! You do need to make sure you get enough sleep, but I see tremendous growth since last week—your hard work paid off! Have you had feedback from your mentor yet?	Reinforcing Effort and Providing Recognition
Wiki	Great! Your team has collected seventeen sources of information about local water contamination sources. What are the common arguments from each side, and who's on each side?	Summarizing and Note Taking; Identifying Similarities and Differences
YouTube	I'm glad you posted your latest revision of your PSA. I like the improvements to the script and how you've "chunked" the interview. However, the editing was a bit choppy or abrupt. You can use the audio to make bridges between scenes that are smoother and set up the viewer for the change. Here's a sample taking your work and using these techniques. Why don't you try remixing and posting the new version for comments?	Setting Objectives and Providing Feedback; Homework and Practice

Assessing Communication (NETS-S2)

Example: In an online journal, what student artifacts might prompt a student to say any of the following in a self-assessment?

- *I analyze my experiences, assumptions, and beliefs to identify areas of growth and learning in skills, strategies, and conceptual understanding.*

- *I write so that I can read and understand what I have written, and if someone else is going to read my journal, I follow standard conventions so the audience can understand my writing.*

Assessing Collaboration (NETS-S2)

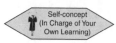

Example: In an online literature circle, what student artifacts might prompt a student to say any of the following in a self-assessment?

- *I simplify complicated ideas.*
- *I stimulate discussion by presenting different points of view.*
- *I request clarification.*
- *I make people feel good about what they contribute to the group.*

Research and Information Fluency (NETS-S3)

The quality of work that students produce depends on both the substance and the processes they use in developing the results. Creativity and Innovation, along with Communication and Collaboration, largely focus on the process side of the equation. The quality of substance (facts, information, ideas) students use to build their products (reports, presentations, essays) depends on the degree to which they've developed their research and information fluency skills. This means not only being able to find the right information and discern its validity but also knowing what to do with it, in terms of organizing it to meet the needs of the task.

For too many students (and their teachers), there is a belief that the answer to every question can be found with Google. The ubiquitous access to Internet searches increases, rather than eliminates, the need for highly developed information literacy skills. Unfortunately, the only teachers who have honed these skills as part of their professional preparation are those who went to library school (library media specialists). This knowledge gap among the rest of us is easily filled with care and attention, and this chapter is devoted to making sure you are well prepared to guide your students in developing these critically important digital age learning skills.

In the curriculum examples that follow, the Knowledge Building activity types from TPACK provide powerful strategies for increasing student engagement, especially when combined with appropriate use of Marzano's high-probability strategies.

> Students apply digital tools to gather, evaluate, and use information. Students:
>
> A. plan strategies to guide inquiry.
>
> B. locate, organize, analyze, evaluate, synthesize, and ethically use information from a variety of sources and media.
>
> C. evaluate and select information sources and digital tools based on the appropriateness to specific tasks.
>
> D. process data and report results.

What Does NETS-S3 (Research and Information Fluency) Challenge Students to Do in English?

Students apply digital tools to gather, evaluate, and use information. Students:

    A. plan strategies to guide inquiry.

Project task: Design a process to collaborate with mentors or peer groups to generate shared questions and lines of inquiry on the topic of aging, as it affects (and will affect) your grandparents, parents, yourself.

New idea: *Where Are the Signposts?* What processes can we use to determine which information is useful in guiding decisions on the path of aging? What are all possible sources of information about the effects of aging on students' grandparents and parents and on themselves?

Which are the best sources (accurate, authentic) of the information we need? How do we find them? How do we accurately summarize and cite the relevant information within these sources?

College and Career Readiness Anchor Standards for Writing

Research to Build and Present Knowledge – Grade 8

- Conduct short as well as more sustained research projects based on focused questions, demonstrating understanding of the subject under investigation.

- Gather relevant information from multiple print and digital sources, assess the credibility and accuracy of each source, and integrate the information while avoiding plagiarism.

- Draw evidence from literary or informational texts to support analysis, reflection, and research.

Learning Strategies

Use Identifying Similarities and Differences to enhance students' understanding of and ability to use knowledge by engaging them in mental processes that involve identifying ways that items are alike and different.

    B. locate, organize, analyze, evaluate, synthesize, and ethically use information from a variety of sources and media.

Project task: In the novel *The Last Book in the Universe*, by Rodman Philbrick, the main character poses the question, "Why bother to read any more if you can just *probe* [experience the world exclusively through virtual "reality"]?" Participate in a panel discussion, giving a reaction to this question from one of these viewpoints: William Shakespeare, a Sony executive in charge of the PlayStation division, a science fiction author, a student of 1990, a student of 2050.

New idea: *Reality—Is It What We Think?* How has our idea of reality changed with the introduction of written language, printed books, radio and TV, digital media and the Internet, and virtual worlds?

College and Career Readiness Anchor Standards for Reading

Key Ideas and Details (Reading Standards for Informational Text) – Grade 8

- Cite the textual evidence that most strongly supports an analysis of what the text says explicitly as well as inferences drawn from the text.

- Determine a central idea of a text and analyze its development over the course of the text, including its relationship to supporting ideas; provide an objective summary of the text.

- Analyze how a text makes connections among and distinctions between individuals, ideas, or events (e.g., through comparisons, analogies, or categories).

Learning Strategies

Use Identifying Similarities and Differences to enhance students' understanding of and ability to use knowledge by engaging them in mental processes that involve identifying ways of knowing and communicating that are alike and different.

C. evaluate and select information sources and digital tools based on the appropriateness to specific tasks.

Project task: Create an audio history presentation (suitable for school broadcast or podcast if possible) by producing audio profiles of students' parents' lives after high school.

New idea: *Family as Primary Sources!* We often think of libraries or Internet searches as the best sources for historical information. However, history not only happens to people but is created one person at a time. For our topic, the first place to turn is right at home.

College and Career Readiness Anchor Standards for Reading

Integration of Knowledge and Ideas (Reading Standards for Informational Text) – Grade 8

- Evaluate the advantages and disadvantages of using different mediums (e.g., print or digital text, video, multimedia) to present a particular topic or idea.

Learning
Strategies

Use Homework and Practice to extend the learning opportunities for students to practice, review, and apply knowledge. Enhance students' ability to reach the expected level of proficiency for designing and conducting audio interviews.

D. process data and report results.

Project task: Participate in face-to-face and online class discussions of peer-reviewed writing to select pieces for a class anthology, then reflect on the effectiveness of each method.

New idea: *One, the Other, or Both?* The effectiveness of online versus face-to-face interactions is often judged as an "either-or," although research suggests that a blended model produces the best results. Structure this activity so that one part of the class does only face-to-face first, another does only online first, and a third part of the class does both from the beginning. Have all students write in their journals about their experiences to provide data for comparison.

College and Career Readiness Anchor Standards for Reading

Integration of Knowledge and Ideas (Reading Standards for Informational Text) – Grade 8

- Evaluate the advantages and disadvantages of using different mediums (e.g., print or digital text, video, multimedia) to present a particular topic or idea.

Learning
Strategies

Use Identifying Similarities and Differences to enhance students' understanding of and ability to use knowledge by engaging them in mental processes that involve identifying ways that face-to-face and online peer review processes are alike and different.

What Does NETS-S3 (Research and Information Fluency) Challenge Students to Do in Math?

Students apply digital tools to gather, evaluate, and use information. Students:

A. plan strategies to guide inquiry.

Project task: Students formulate questions related to their physical environment and how similar needs are met in two contrasting populations or cultures, by designing studies that can answer the questions, collecting appropriate data, and presenting conclusions.

New idea: *Start Where You Are!* By examining how selected needs are met in our community, students can establish a baseline for comparison with other populations or cultures. Guiding questions may include What are all possible sources of information about the selected physical environmental characteristics in contrasting populations or cultures? Which are the best sources (accurate, authentic)? How do we find them? How do we accurately summarize and cite the relevant information within these sources?

Learning Strategies

Use Cues, Questions, and Advance Organizers to enhance students' ability to retrieve, use, and organize what they already know about the selected physical environmental characteristics in contrasting populations or cultures.

B. locate, organize, analyze, evaluate, synthesize, and ethically use information from a variety of sources and media.

Project task: Measure and compare the amount of time spent in school and at home doing homework, watching TV, playing video games, and communicating with friends (using cell phones, the Internet, and so on). Create graphical representations of data using graphing calculators, spreadsheets, and other data visualization tools.

New idea: *Design a Data Gathering Strategy!* Students today often do more than one thing at a time (for example, doing homework while listening to music, IM'ing friends and searching the Internet), making it a real challenge to gather data. What are all possible sources of information about how students spend their time?

Common Core State Standards

Mathematical Practices (Grade 8)

1. Make sense of problems and persevere in solving them.

2. Reason abstractly and quantitatively.

3. Construct viable arguments and critique the reasoning of others.

4. Model with mathematics.

Common Core State Standards – Math Grade 8

Statistics and Probability – 8.SP

- Investigate patterns of association in bivariate data.

Learning
Strategies

Use Summarizing and Note Taking to enhance students' ability to synthesize information and organize it in a way that captures the main ideas and supporting details.

C. evaluate and select information sources and digital tools based on the appropriateness to specific tasks.

Project task: Determine the effects of an increasing student population on existing school bus capacity, routes, and schedules, using mathematical understanding and problem-solving processes to collaboratively identify problems.

New idea: *How Are Schedules Built?* Simple arithmetic (taking the number of new students and dividing by the number of students each bus can transport) will not do. Students of different ages attend different schools, which start at different times. One surprising discovery from looking at data is that most school start times are determined by sports practice schedules. These problems are addressed in every school district in the nation. What can be learned from others? Guiding questions to use with your students may include What are all possible sources of information about the effects of an increasing student population on existing school bus capacity, routes, and schedules? Which are the best sources (accurate, authentic) that provide the information we need?

Learning
Strategies

Use Summarizing and Note Taking to enhance students' ability to synthesize information and organize it in a way that captures the main ideas and supporting details.

D. process data and report results.

Project task: Investigate whether local recycling efforts help conserve energy and natural resources and what proportion of the recycled materials are used in various items, by incorporating math concepts into a community service project.

New idea: *Follow the Trail!* This stuff we use—where does it all come from? Where does it all go? It takes lots of math to calculate the energy that goes into creating, transporting, disposing of, or recycling the materials we use every day. Guiding questions to use with your students may include What are all possible sources of information about

> **Common Core State Standards – Math Grade 8**
>
> **Expressions and Equations – 8.EE**
>
> - Work with radicals and integer exponents.
> - Understand the connections between proportional relationships, lines, and linear equations.
> - Analyze and solve linear equations and pairs of simultaneous linear equations.

> **Common Core State Standards – Math Grade 8**
>
> **Functions – 8.F**
>
> - Define, evaluate, and compare functions.
> - Use functions to model relationships between quantities.

Eyes on the Prize!

the effectiveness of local recycling efforts? Which are the best sources (accurate, authentic) that provide the information we need?

Learning
Strategies

Use Cues, Questions, and Advance Organizers to enhance students' ability to retrieve, use, and organize what they already know about the energy that goes into recycling.

What Does NETS-S3 (Research and Information Fluency) Challenge Students to Do in Science?

Students apply digital tools to gather, evaluate, and use information. Students:

    A. *plan strategies to guide inquiry.*

Project task: Investigate the possible relationships between variations in weather, performance of school sports teams, and moods of students, by executing the steps of scientific inquiry.

New idea: *Harvest the Data!* Gathering data about local weather over time is simple, as online databases exist. Similarly, school sports team data are kept for every event. Finding data on student moods represents more of a challenge. What research techniques are best for each task? What are all possible sources of information on the possible relationships between variations in weather, performance of school sports teams, and moods of students? Which are the best sources (accurate, authentic) of the information we need? How do we find them? How do we accurately summarize and cite the relevant information within these sources?

Science Activity Type: Conceptual Knowledge Building

(Data Analysis)

Students describe relationships, understand cause-and-effect, prioritize evidence, determine possible sources of error/discrepancies, etc.

Learning Strategies

Use Summarizing and Note Taking to enhance students' ability to synthesize information and organize it in a way that captures the main ideas and supporting details.

    B. *locate, organize, analyze, evaluate, synthesize, and ethically use information from a variety of sources and media.*

Project task: Investigate whether local recycling efforts help conserve energy and natural resources, using a broad range of tools and techniques to plan and conduct an inquiry to address the question. (Science Strand: science in personal and social perspectives) *Note:* for a multidisciplinary unit, this task can be paired with a math project based on the same scenario.

New idea: *Buried Facts?* How can we find out what's in the dump, or what would have been there if not for recycling? What are all possible sources of information about results of local recycling efforts? Which are the best sources (accurate, authentic) of the information we need? How do we find them? How do we accurately summarize and cite the relevant information within these sources?

Science Activity Type: Procedural Knowledge Building

(Record Data)

Students record observational and recorded data in tables, graphs, images, lab notes

Learning Strategies

Use Cooperative Learning to provide students with opportunities to interact with each other in groups in ways that enhance their learning, by conducting first-person observations and interviewing professionals who work in the recycling industry.

C. evaluate and select information sources and digital tools based on the appropriateness to specific tasks.

Project task: Communicate the procedures and results of an investigation that evaluates and compares the quality of local water from different sources by performing simple tests (for example, for pH, salinity, hardness, temperature, turbidity), using a variety of media tools to make oral and written presentations, which include written notes and descriptions, drawings, photos, and charts. (Science Strand: Earth and space science)

New idea: *Build an Information Reservoir!* As information flows in, make sure that students learn to organize it in ways that make it easier to analyze and present the findings. What are all possible sources of information about evaluating the quality of local water from different sources? Which are the best sources (accurate, authentic) of the information we need? How do we find them? How do we accurately summarize and cite the relevant information within these sources?

Science Activity Type: Knowledge Expression

(Do a Presentation or Demonstration)

Students present or demonstrate laboratory or research findings, or other course learning (e.g., a system of the human body).

Learning Strategies

Use Summarizing and Note Taking to enhance students' ability to synthesize information and organize it in a way that captures the main ideas and supporting details.

D. process data and report results.

Project task: Collaborate with a network of learners to investigate the societal, ecological, and political issues surrounding the availability of drinkable water, using a variety of digital collaboration tools. (Science Strand: science in personal and social perspectives)

New idea: *Can We Make a Difference? Best Ideas Festival!* Consider participation in H2O for Life (http://www.h2oforlifeschools.org/). H2O for Life partners schools, youth groups, businesses, faith organizations, clubs, and individuals with schools in developing nations in need of water, sanitation, and hygiene education. In one example project, WASH in Schools, donor partners learn of the global water crisis through service learning, outreach, and other educational avenues while raising funds to sponsor a WASH project at their recipient partner school. Students and adults learn that they can make a difference in the lives of others by becoming energized global citizens and activists for change.

As a follow-up, present a public panel outlining the global situation and debating local actions that can help make sure your community has adequate and reliable sources of drinking water now and into the future.

Science Activity Type: Knowledge Expression

(Debate)

Students discuss opposing viewpoints embedded in science content knowledge, linked to ethics, nature of science, personal preferences, politics, etc.

Learning Strategies

Use Reinforcing Effort and Providing Recognition to enhance students' understanding of the relationship between effort and achievement by addressing students' attitudes and beliefs about learning. Provide students with rewards or praise for their accomplishments related to researching and presenting findings on the importance of access to drinkable water.

What Does NETS-S3 (Research and Information Fluency) Challenge Students to Do in Geography?

Students apply digital tools to gather, evaluate, and use information. Students:

A. *plan strategies to guide inquiry.*

Project task: Write a dialogue and storyboard a video about conflicts between a farmer and a city water board administrator about the use of regional water resources.

New idea: *Walk in Their Shoes!* Organize student teams to research the arguments that are opposite to their views to develop realistic characters for both sides of the controversy. Then repeat the process from the other character's point of view, in order to develop material for the video storyboard.

What are all the possible sources for information about the different issues a farmer and a city water board administrator face about the use of regional water resources? Which are the best sources (accurate, authentic) of the information we need? How do we find them? How do we accurately summarize and cite the relevant information within these sources?

Geography Activity Type: Knowledge Building

(Compare/Contrast)

Students interrogate information to understand multiple characteristics, evidence, and/or perspectives on a topic.

Learning Strategies

Use Cooperative Learning to provide students with opportunities to interact with each other in groups in ways that enhance their learning.

B. *locate, organize, analyze, evaluate, synthesize, and ethically use information from a variety of sources and media.*

Project task: Develop a community response plan in the event of a natural disaster, working collaboratively on a team using a geographic information system (GIS) to develop models.

New idea: *Work with Professionals!* Each community has volunteer or professional first responders, as well as public safety staff. Work in teams to gather information from these people and to research existing emergency response plans from communities facing similar risks.

What are all the possible sources for information about developing a community response plan in the event of a natural disaster? Which are the best sources (accurate, authentic) of the information we need? How do we find them? How do we accurately summarize and cite the relevant information within these sources?

Geography Activity Type: Knowledge Building

(Engage in Data-Based Inquiry)

Using student-generated data or print-based and digital data available online, students pursue original lines of inquiry.

Learning Strategies

Use Cooperative Learning to provide students with opportunities to interact with each other in groups in ways that enhance their learning.

C. evaluate and select information sources and digital tools based on the appropriateness to specific tasks.

Project task: Work on a team to write and create a video about immigrants to a new country struggling to deal with the issues involved in adapting to an unfamiliar environment.

New idea: *Use Primary Sources!* Many immigrants who've overcome the challenges of moving to a different culture have captured their experiences in diaries, journals, letters, and biographies. Use these primary sources, and collaborate with students from the original cultures of the immigrants who are the subject of the video.

What are all the possible sources of information about the issues immigrants face in adapting to an unfamiliar environment? Which are the best sources (accurate, authentic) of the information we need? How do we find them? How do we accurately summarize and cite the relevant information within these sources?

Geography Activity Type: Knowledge Building

(Engage in Artifact-Based Inquiry)

- Students explore a topic using physical or virtual artifacts, including data, text, images, etc.

- Face to face, via audio/videoconference, or via email, students question someone on a chosen topic; may be digitally recorded and shared.

Learning Strategies

Use Summarizing and Note Taking to enhance students' ability to synthesize information and organize it in a way that captures the main ideas and supporting details.

D. process data and report results.

Project task: Compose an email message to a local or state official stating your opinion on a relevant community issue (for example, suggesting the location of a new community recreation area and supporting the suggestion with factual information).

New idea: *Research Realities!* Recommendations require supporting data that are complete and accurate. In the case of a proposed community recreation area, for example, what are the facts about the issue directly affecting students? Use a similar research process for any student-selected community issue. What are all the possible sources for the selected community issue? What are all possible sources for writing effective advocacy communications to local or state officials? Which are the best sources (accurate, authentic) of the information we need? How do we find them? How do we accurately summarize and cite the relevant information within these sources?

Geography Activity Type: Convergent Knowledge Expression

(Engage in Data-Based Inquiry)

Using student-generated data or print-based and digital data available online, students pursue original lines of inquiry.

Learning
Strategies

Use Summarizing and Note Taking to enhance students' ability to synthesize information and organize it in a way that captures the main ideas and supporting details.

Doug Johnson: Insights on Information Fluency

Doug Johnson is the director of media and technology for the Mankato (Minnesota) Public Schools. His teaching experience has included work in grades K–12. He is the author of five books, a long-running column in Library Media Connection, *the Blue Skunk Blog, and articles in over forty books and periodicals. The following material is from transcripts of a video interview. Clips from this video interview are also available on the DVD that accompanies this book.*

On Moving from Content Experts to Process Experts

When the Internet first came into our schools in Mankato, I was at an elementary library, and I came up behind three or four fifth-grade boys that were sitting around the Internet terminal, and they were giggling, and you never know—it always makes me nervous whenever I see kids giggling at an Internet terminal. But anyway, I came up behind, and I looked over their shoulder, and they were at the Center for Disease Control in Atlanta, looking up information about the Ebola virus.

Obviously, what had happened is they'd seen a show or read a book or looked at a magazine article, and if you know anything about Ebola, it's a good, gory disease, so it was just right up the interest alley of fifth-grade boys. And I thought about that, and on my way home, I started thinking more and more about how that's going to change the dynamic of the classroom.

Traditionally, the teacher has been the dispenser of information. If you want to know something, you go to the textbook, you go to the teacher, and if they don't know it, well, it doesn't need to be known. But suddenly you've got three fifth-grade boys that are coming back into a classroom. . . . Who becomes the content expert in that particular case?

Well, it's shifted, hasn't it? And if you're a classroom teacher who retains their identity by saying, I'm the dispenser of all things that need to be known, you're in for a world of hurt, all right? But what a lot of teachers now are finding out, because kids have access to so much information, is that instead of being content experts, they have to become process experts.

So when those kids come back into the classroom, they have people that ask questions like, where did you get this information? How do you know that information is reliable? Is this information important to the other people in the class or in the community? And if it's important, how are you going to let other people know that? And finally, how are you going to know you've done a good job of that?

Those are all process kinds of questions, and those are the kinds of questions the librarians have always been good at and those are the kinds of questions that librarians, I think, are going to have to help coach teachers with or help partner with teachers over, help teachers become good at. I mean, that's kind of a pioneering role.

On Redefining Research

It's not just the library, but I think the entire nature of research we see has to change. David Loertscher (past president of the American Association of School Librarians) is one of the experts in our field, and he calls them "Ban Those Birds Units" (www.davidvl.org/Achieve /Ban_Birds_Action_Research.pdf), where you pick a bird and you go out and you talk about his color and its habitat and things like that.

Where we're seeing the most viable and worthwhile kind of research being done, it has some different characteristics. First, it's authentic research. You're not out looking for the right answer. You're out trying to answer a question that neither the student nor the teacher really knows the answer to, which makes it a lot more interesting for the teacher actually as well too, because you're not fishing for the one right answer. You're really generally trying to answer questions or solve a problem that doesn't have a set answer.

The other thing is we're finding that with this generation of students, relevance, relevance, relevance is so critical. In order to make research relevant, students have to have a great deal more choice than they would have had to have had in the past. So pick a real question, pick a question that has interest and relevance to you, that's certainly another thing.

The third thing is how you evaluate the process, so authentic assessment—making sure teachers have good authentic assessment tools that help guide students to let them know when they've done a good job and when they haven't—is important as well.

The other thing that I see a lot of good teachers and media specialists doing now is emphasizing the importance of primary resources, not just the secondary resources that you traditionally find in libraries that have already been embedded.

So they're having kids do experiments. They're having kids do interviews. They're having kids look at source documents. They're having kids do surveys and all of those kinds of things. And that's another area that I think causes a lot of discomfort for teachers, because they themselves have never been asked to do primary research: maybe researching their master's thesis might have been the first time they were asked to look outside of using previously digested material, we might call it.

So I think to help teachers get over their anxiety about that, I think you actually have to try that once and if you try it once, you're going to find out that kids are so much more receptive, so much more excited about the research process than having to do those bird units. So hopefully your students will pick areas that have real meaning for them, and you're going to get a great product as a result.

> ### Defining Information, Communications, and Technology (ICT) Literacy
>
> Here is the definition from the Programme for International Student Assessment (PISA) ICT expert panel: [ICT] literacy is the interest, attitude and ability of individuals to appropriately use digital technology and communication tools to access, manage, integrate and evaluate information, construct new knowledge, and communicate with others in order to participate effectively in society.

Assessing Research and Information Fluency (NETS-S3)

Let's examine all six ICT competencies, along with sample tasks that demonstrate these skills.

Access (knowing about and knowing how to collect and retrieve information)

Sample tasks:

- Open a file, email message, or application
- Access information using a browser through the World Wide Web
- Navigate within a website to locate information
- Use a search engine within an application or Web page

Manage (organizing information into existing classification schemes)

Sample tasks:

- Manage files (save to specific locations, change locations)
- Organize and paste information into a table or chart
- Enter information into simulation software
- Enter information into a database
- Use a word processor to create an ordered list of items

Integrate (interpreting, summarizing, comparing, and contrasting information using similar or different forms of representation)

Sample tasks:

- Compare information presented in a video clip and graph
- Look through several websites to identify, compare, and summarize information on a particular topic

Evaluate (reflecting to make judgments about the quality, relevance, usefulness, or efficiency of information)

Sample tasks:

- Select websites that best meet specified criteria
- Evaluate reliability of information sources
- Use a simulation to pick a correct hypothesis

Construct (generating new information and knowledge by adapting, applying, designing, inventing, representing, or authoring information)

Sample tasks:

- Write a brief email message

- Write a paper using a word processor

- Develop a report using presentation software

- Create a Web page

- Transform one representation to another, for instance a table to a graph

Communicate (conveying information and knowledge to various individuals or groups)

Sample tasks:

- Send a message (email, instant message)

- Contribute to an online discussion on a mailing list, forum, wiki, or blog

- Research and recommend purchase of an item using e-commerce

- Make a multimedia presentation

Critical Thinking, Problem Solving, and Decision Making (NETS-S4)

Critical thinking is the greatest deficit cited by employers regarding the abilities of students seeking jobs.

If it takes ten thousand hours of practice to reach mastery, an outside observer would think that the purpose of schools was to prepare students to become professional test-takers. The amount of instructional time devoted to learning and developing 21st century skills (collectively comprising the specific skills of problem identification, strategies for problem solving, and sequencing challenges of ever-increasing complexity) is clearly not sufficient to counter the existing imbalance.

This section will acquaint you with project examples that develop and strengthen these skills, as well as strategies you can use to assess growth in these critical areas.

Students use critical thinking skills to plan and conduct research, manage projects, solve problems, and make informed decisions using appropriate digital tools and resources. Students:

A. identify and define authentic problems and significant questions for investigation.

B. plan and manage activities to develop a solution or complete a project.

C. collect and analyze data to identify solutions and/or make informed decisions.

D. use multiple processes and diverse perspectives to explore alternative solutions.

What Does NETS-S4 (Critical Thinking, Problem Solving, and Decision Making) Challenge Students to Do in English?

Students use critical thinking skills to plan and conduct research, manage projects, solve problems, and make informed decisions using appropriate digital tools and resources. Students:

A. identify and define authentic problems and significant questions for investigation.

Project task: Design a process to collaborate with mentors or peer groups to generate shared questions and lines of inquiry on the topic of aging, as it affects (and will affect) your grandparents, parents, yourself.

New idea: *Great Expectations?* The U.S. Census Bureau's view on the future of longevity is that life expectancy in the United States will be in the mideighties by 2050 (up from 77.85 in 2006) and will top out eventually in the low nineties, barring major scientific advances that can change the rate of human aging itself, as opposed to merely treating the effects of aging, as is done today. The Census Bureau also predicted that the United States would have 5.3 million people over the age of one hundred in 2100. The United Nations has also made projections far out into the future, up to 2300, at which point it projects that life expectancies in most developed countries will be between 100 and 106 years and still rising, though more and more slowly than before.[7]

How have advancements in medicine, technology, and knowledge about aging changed the prospects for present and future generations?

College and Career Readiness Anchor Standards for Writing

Research to Build and Present Knowledge – Grade 8

- Conduct short as well as more sustained research projects based on focused questions, demonstrating understanding of the subject under investigation.

- Gather relevant information from multiple print and digital sources, assess the credibility and accuracy of each source, and integrate the information while avoiding plagiarism.

- Draw evidence from literary or informational texts to support analysis, reflection, and research.

Learning
Strategies

Use Generating and Testing Hypotheses to enhance students' understanding of and ability to use knowledge by engaging them in mental processes that involve making and testing hypotheses about what lies ahead with respect to aging.

B. plan and manage activities to develop a solution or complete a project.

Project task: Using a topic of interest (based on units covered in science, social studies, history, or math classes), create an annotated bibliography of important resource materials (books, newspapers, magazines, online sources, video, music, and so on). Include a working bibliography of sources consulted or skimmed but not selected. (*Note:* It is OK to use the previous topic of longevity implications, too!)

New idea: *Team Research!* All peer-reviewed books, reports, and articles contain lists of the sources used (bibliographies). Combining and sharing annotated bibliographies created by groups requires effective strategies for organizing the work. Social bookmarking tools (such as de.liciou.us) can be particularly useful in team research.

College and Career Readiness Anchor Standards for Reading

Integration of Knowledge and Ideas (Reading Standards for Informational Text) – Grade 8

- Evaluate the advantages and disadvantages of using different mediums (e.g., print or digital text, video, multimedia) to present a particular topic or idea.

- Delineate and evaluate the argument and specific claims in a text, assessing whether the reasoning is sound and the evidence is relevant and sufficient; recognize when irrelevant evidence is introduced.

- Analyze a case in which two or more texts provide conflicting information on the same topic and identify where the texts disagree on matters of fact or interpretation.

Learning Strategies

Use Cooperative Learning to provide students with opportunities to interact with each other in groups in ways that enhance their learning. High-quality student research can provide valuable clues for students who wish to create high-quality products from the assignments they are given.

C. collect and analyze data to identify solutions and/or make informed decisions.

Project task: Solve a mini-mystery with each group member having only a small piece of the information, and analyze the effectiveness of the interaction in group problem solving.

New idea: *Be Einstein!* In the Vanishing Videos forensic problem-solving activity (http://www.wiredsafety.org/wiredlearning/Einstein/index.html), Art Wolinsky has updated a puzzle created by Albert Einstein. At the time he created it, Einstein estimated that only about 2 percent of the world's population would be able to solve it. This project introduces a variety of problem-solving strategies, including defining the problem, organizing information, identifying important information, combining information, identifying by process of elimination, recognizing visual patterns, and using a solution matrix.

Learning Strategies

Use Generating and Testing Hypotheses to enhance students' understanding of and ability to use knowledge by engaging them in mental processes that involve making and testing hypotheses. Document the strategies (both successful and unsuccessful) used in solving Vanishing Videos.

D. use multiple processes and diverse perspectives to explore alternative solutions.

Project task: Challenge students to complete a collaborative research project about a topic of their choice regarding changes to policies governing school technology use, using online research.

New idea: *Protect? Promote? Prevent? Digital Dilemmas!* School policies determine what is possible with school technology and what is not. Many factors contribute to shaping how networks and computers are set up to promote learning while protecting students and systems from dangers and preventing abuses by users. Online searches, blogs, wikis, email discussions, and Skype conversations can all connect students with peers, experts, and others who are responsible for developing school technology policies and how these shape learning. All policies have consequences, some intended and some unforeseen. The same is true of changes to policies, which can have a domino effect. Where should the balance be, from the perspectives of students, teachers, administrators, technology coordinators, parents, and the community?

College and Career Readiness Anchor Standards for Reading

Integration of Knowledge and Ideas (Reading Standards for Informational Text) – Grade 8

- Evaluate the advantages and disadvantages of using different mediums (e.g., print or digital text, video, multimedia) to present a particular topic or idea.

- Delineate and evaluate the argument and specific claims in a text, assessing whether the reasoning is sound and the evidence is relevant and sufficient; recognize when irrelevant evidence is introduced.

- Analyze a case in which two or more texts provide conflicting information on the same topic and identify where the texts disagree on matters of fact or interpretation.

Learning Strategies

Use Generating and Testing Hypotheses to enhance students' understanding of and ability to use knowledge by engaging them in mental processes that involve making and testing hypotheses about each proposed change to school technology policies.

What Does NETS•S4 (Critical Thinking, Problem Solving, and Decision Making) Challenge Students to Do in Math?

Students use critical thinking skills to plan and conduct research, manage projects, solve problems, and make informed decisions using appropriate digital tools and resources. Students:

A. *identify and define authentic problems and significant questions for investigation.*

Project task: Redesign your school to rely entirely on renewable energy sources, using computation, customary and metric measurements, scale factors, ratios, and proportions.

New idea: *Think Green!* Find out what energy it takes to run the school now. Research what alternatives exist now, and which are under development. Introduce materials from the U.S. Department of Energy's Energy Efficiency and Renewable Energy website (http://www.eere.energy.gov/education/lessonplans/) and incorporate the findings into this activity. What are the most feasible and easily accomplished changes that can be made now? What redesign processes have worked in other schools?

Learning Strategies

Use Generating and Testing Hypotheses to enhance students' understanding of and ability to use knowledge by engaging them in mental processes that involve making and testing hypotheses.

B. *plan and manage activities to develop a solution or complete a project.*

Project task: Select and apply appropriate problem-solving strategies to collaboratively plan, in an online group, all aspects of an upcoming eighth-grade dance or prom.

New idea: *Make a Plan, Work the Plan!* Your event will require people, money, and things (for example, equipment, decorations, entertainment, food). Some of these may be donated; for others, fundraising may be needed. You need to know what you have in order to know what you still need. Using the information available, put your team to work in developing a strategy to get the resources you need and the people you'll need to prepare everything in advance.

Learning Strategies

Use Cooperative Learning to provide students with opportunities to interact with each other in groups in ways that enhance their learning.

> **Common Core State Standards**
>
> **Mathematical Practices (Grade 8)**
>
> 1. Make sense of problems and persevere in solving them.
> 2. Reason abstractly and quantitatively.
> 3. Construct viable arguments and critique the reasoning of others.
> 4. Model with mathematics.

> **Common Core State Standards**
>
> **Mathematical Practices (Grade 8)**
>
> 1. Make sense of problems and persevere in solving them.
> 2. Reason abstractly and quantitatively.

Students combine information from multiple sources to develop their plan, and they distribute work to their team members.

C. collect and analyze data to identify solutions and/or make informed decisions.

Project task: Using the previous analysis of the effects of an increasing student population on existing school bus capacity, collaboratively use mathematical understanding and problem-solving processes to identify possible solutions. (See the example for NETS-S3 in Math on page 90 for the previous analysis task.)

New idea: *Develop Choices!* Based on how various factors are prioritized, some alternatives look better than others. For example, although research shows that high school students perform better with a later start in the day, few schools use later start times.

Learning Strategies

Use Generating and Testing Hypotheses to enhance students' understanding of and ability to use knowledge by engaging them in mental processes that involve making and testing hypotheses. Determine the effects of an increasing student population on existing school bus capacity, routes, and schedules, using mathematical understanding and problem-solving processes to collaboratively identify problems and suggest solutions.

D. use multiple processes and diverse perspectives to explore alternative solutions.

Project task: Using the previous analysis of the effects of an increasing student population on existing school bus capacity, collaboratively use mathematical understanding and problem-solving processes to identify possible solutions.

New idea: *Draw New Maps!* Many decisions about bus schedules are made without public input, and for efficiency rather than educational reasons. Show the number of students on each bus, new routes, and timings for each solution.

Learning Strategies

Use Nonlinguistic Representation to enhance students' ability to represent and elaborate on knowledge using

> ## Common Core State Standards – Math Grade 8
>
> ### Functions – 8.F
>
> - Define, evaluate, and compare functions.
> - Use functions to model relationships between quantities.

> ## Common Core State Standards
>
> ### Mathematical Practices (Grade 8)
>
> 1. Make sense of problems and persevere in solving them.
> 2. Reason abstractly and quantitatively.
> 3. Construct viable arguments and critique the reasoning of others.
> 4. Model with mathematics.
> 5. Use appropriate tools strategically.
> 6. Attend to precision.
> 7. Look for and make use of structure.
> 8. Look for and express regularity in repeated reasoning.

mental images. If possible, develop animated maps to show the problems and alternative solutions.

What Does NETS-S4 (Critical Thinking, Problem Solving, and Decision Making) Challenge Students to Do in Science?

Students use critical thinking skills to plan and conduct research, manage projects, solve problems, and make informed decisions using appropriate digital tools and resources. Students:

A. identify and define authentic problems and significant questions for investigation.

B. plan and manage activities to develop a solution or complete a project.

C. collect and analyze data to identify solutions and/or make informed decisions.

D. use multiple processes and diverse perspectives to explore alternative solutions.

For this example in Science, we will use a single project, based on the universal need for clean, safe water, to illustrate all four elements of this standard. Because this project idea connects global challenges with local action, it provides the opportunity to move from "start to finish," from designing an approach to implementing data gathering and analysis, resulting in recommendations for local action.

Project task (a): Collaborate with a network of learners to investigate the societal, ecological, and political issues surrounding the availability of drinkable water, using a variety of digital collaboration tools.

New idea: *What If We Run Dry?* It's been predicted that conflict over drinkable water will be more important than conflict over oil in the 21st century. Where are problems likely to happen first? What can be done to prevent problems? How do we investigate the societal, ecological, and political issues surrounding the availability of drinkable water? For resources, links, and background information, visit H2O for Life (http://www.h2oforlifeschools.org/).

A. identify and define authentic problems and significant questions for investigation.

In the first phase, identifying authentic problems, we must guide students to leverage their preexisting knowledge and develop predictions.

Science Activity Type: Conceptual Knowledge Building

(Develop Predictions, Hypotheses, Questions, Variables)

Students develop and think about predictions, and select pertinent hypotheses, testable questions, and variables.

Learning
Strategies

Use Generating and Testing Hypotheses to enhance students' understanding of and ability to use knowledge by engaging them in mental processes that involve making and testing hypotheses.

B. plan and manage activities to develop a solution or complete a project.

In the second phase, we need to develop a plan for the investigation, assign roles, and make sure that students understand and are prepared to perform these roles.

Project task (b): Develop a plan for an investigation that evaluates and compares the quality of local water from different sources by performing simple tests (for example, for pH, salinity, hardness, temperature, turbidity), using a variety of media tools to make oral and written presentations, which include written notes and descriptions, drawings, photos, and charts. (Science Strand: Earth and space science)

C. collect and analyze data to identify solutions and/or make informed decisions.

In the third phase, students implement the plan, including gathering and interacting with data as a basis for developing solutions.

Project tasks (c and d): Communicate the procedures and results of an investigation that evaluates and compares the quality of local water from different sources by performing simple tests (for example, for pH, salinity, hardness, temperature, turbidity), using a variety of media tools to make oral and written presentations, which include written notes and descriptions, drawings, photos, and charts. (Science Strand: Earth and space science)

New idea: *Help Keep Our Water Clean!* How do we perform simple tests (for example, for pH, salinity, hardness, temperature, turbidity) to evaluate and compare the quality of local water from different sources? If the results show that water is of uniformly high quality, what needs to be done to keep it that way? If there are problems, what may be the contributing causes? What needs to be done to improve quality in these locations?

Science Activity Type: Procedural Knowledge Building

(Observe, Collect Samples, Do Procedures, Record Data)

- Students make observations from physical or digital experiences.

- Students obtain samples/items to study (water, soil, video footage).

- Students run trials or otherwise carry out steps to investigations.

- Students record observational and recorded data in tables, graphs, images, lab notes.

Learning
Strategies

Use Generating and Testing Hypotheses to enhance students' understanding of and ability to use knowledge by engaging them in mental processes that involve making and testing hypotheses.

D. use multiple processes and diverse perspectives to explore alternative solutions.

Eyes on the Prize!

New idea: *Solving Wicked Problems Takes Many Hands.* "Wicked problem" is a term originally used in social planning to describe a problem that is difficult or impossible to solve because of incomplete, contradictory, and changing requirements that are often difficult to recognize. Moreover, because of complex interdependencies, the effort to solve one aspect of a wicked problem may reveal or create other problems.[8] At first look, it is almost inconceivable to find anyone who would be against safe water supplies and in favor of practices that poison this precious resource. However, when we consider how the required changes in agriculture and industry practices would result in costs that are not presently accounted for, we can begin to understand the lack of global progress on this issue. These multiple perspectives need to be taken into account for any scalable and sustained solutions to work.

Science Activity Type: Knowledge Expression

(Do a Presentation/Demonstration, Debate)

- Students present or demonstrate laboratory or research findings, or other course learning (e.g. interdependency of safe water supplies).

- Students discuss opposing viewpoints embedded in science content knowledge, linked to ethics, nature of science, personal preferences, politics, etc.

Learning Strategies

Use Generating and Testing Hypotheses to enhance students' understanding of and ability to use knowledge by engaging them in mental processes that involve making and testing hypotheses.

Assessing Critical Thinking, Problem Solving, and Decision Making (NETS-S4)

Self-concept (In Charge of Your Own Learning)

Example: What student artifacts might prompt a student to say any of the following in a self-assessment?

- *I use my own experiences, knowledge of the content and conventions, and tools of the subject matter to make inferences about new information I am learning.*

- *I keep my mind open after I form an opinion and change it when I find new and important evidence.*

- *I use analysis and cause-and-effect thinking to generate several reasonable options for decisions, to weigh their benefits and drawbacks, and to make informed decisions.*

- *I use inductive and deductive reasoning to identify, describe, and solve problems thoroughly and quickly. I use logical reasoning to identify, describe, and solve problems.*

Digital Citizenship (NETS-S5)

When we launch our well-designed, well-crafted PBL vessel on its way, the driving question serves as the wind in our sails. We reach the shores of relevance, where the size of the audience is in direct proportion to how well we've let the community know what we're up to. If you have an inspiring project, in a sense you have an ethical responsibility to let the community know. If inspiration is not enough for you, there is research to support the importance of relevance.

One thing we've learned in the past couple of decades of online learning is that students respond to a real audience with far more engagement than they demonstrate in a traditional classroom. This "authenticity effect" is harnessed every time you connect the real world back to what's being learned. When student public service announcements are aired on the local-access cable TV channel, motivation takes a quantum leap. When

> Students understand human, cultural, and societal issues related to technology and practice legal and ethical behavior. Students:
>
> A. advocate and practice safe, legal, and responsible use of information and technology.
>
> B. exhibit a positive attitude toward using technology that supports collaboration, learning, and productivity.
>
> C. demonstrate personal responsibility for lifelong learning.
>
> D. exhibit leadership for digital citizenship.

oral histories are woven together with current and old photographs of your town and become a DVD that is shown at a community debut, complete with red carpet, town pride is a rising tide that raises many generations. It doesn't matter which direction you've picked, as long as the driving question you've developed is real.

Preparing to engage an audience while helping students prepare their exhibition of learning or products may seem like raising the stakes, but the rewards are worth the risk.

However, there is some preparation we ourselves need to do. I strongly suggest to teachers, parents, students, and school leaders that they begin their "due diligence" at WiredSafety .org (http://www.wiredsafety.org/).

Originating in 1995 as a group of volunteers rating websites, WiredSafety now provides one-to-one help, extensive information, and education to cyberspace users of all ages on a myriad of Internet and interactive technology safety issues. These services are offered through a worldwide organization composed entirely of volunteers who administer specialized websites and programs. WiredSafety volunteers range in age from eighteen to eighty and run the gamut from TV personalities, teachers, law enforcement officers, PhDs, writers, and librarians to stay-at-home moms, retired persons, and students.

The following resources have been developed by Art Wolinsky, educational technology director for WiredSafety, and are used with his permission.

For educators, the best place to start is at the educator index, where you'll find a host of activities and lessons: http://www.wiredsafety.org/wiredlearning/toc.html.

For students, you'll want to direct their attention to specific activities designed for them: http://www.wiredsafety.org/youth.html.

With this preparation, you and your students are ready to address the following standards:

College and Career Readiness Anchor Standards for Reading

Integration of Knowledge and Ideas (Reading Standards for Informational Text) – Grade 8

- Evaluate the advantages and disadvantages of using different mediums (e.g., print or digital text, video, multimedia) to present a particular topic or idea.

- Delineate and evaluate the argument and specific claims in a text, assessing whether the reasoning is sound and the evidence is relevant and sufficient; recognize when irrelevant evidence is introduced.

- Analyze a case in which two or more texts provide conflicting information on the same topic and identify where the texts disagree on matters of fact or interpretation.

What Does NETS-S5 (Digital Citizenship) Challenge Students to Do in English?

Students understand human, cultural, and societal issues related to technology and practice legal and ethical behavior. Students:

A. advocate and practice safe, legal, and responsible use of information and technology.

Project task: Complete a collaborative research project about a student-selected topic regarding changes to policies governing school technology use, using online research.

New idea: *Safe or Useful? Finding a Balance!* Complete security requires locking computers and networks down so tight that they become useless. Complete openness raises significant privacy, safety, and legal issues.

Learning Strategies

Use Reinforcing Effort and Providing Recognition to enhance students' understanding of the relationship between effort and achievement by addressing students' attitudes and beliefs about learning. Provide students with rewards or praise for their accomplishments related to developing research-based suggestions for changes to school technology policy.

B. exhibit a positive attitude toward using technology that supports collaboration, learning, and productivity.

Project task: Create a class survey on the various communication methods that class members have used outside school in the last month; identify and explain observed patterns.

New idea: *Ask the Students!* Because there is no external measure or assessment of positive attitude, we need to go to the source. Using online tools (email, blogs, portfolios) to capture student reflections about how this experience shapes their feelings about collaboration, learning, and productivity provides a way of making growth visible over time.

College and Career Readiness Anchor Standards for Writing

Production and Distribution of Writing – Grade 8

- Produce clear and coherent writing in which the development, organization, and style are appropriate to task, purpose, and audience.

- Develop and strengthen writing as needed by planning, revising, editing, rewriting, or trying a new approach.

- Use technology, including the Internet, to produce and publish writing and to interact and collaborate with others.

Use Reinforcing Effort and Providing Recognition to enhance students' understanding of the relationship between effort and achievement. Provide students with rewards or praise for their accomplishments related to the attainment of a goal, by sharing (with permission) exemplary student reflections with the wider community.

C. demonstrate personal responsibility for lifelong learning.

Project task: Access real-time global news through technology to stay informed of current events, and create a presentation that compares the detail and timeliness of reporting of the same events in traditional media (print, television, radio).

New idea: *Stay Current, Stay Accurate!* Our interconnected world provides immediacy to our experience of events no matter where they happen, day or night. Our desire to know everything that's happening right up to the minute must be balanced by a desire to ensure that the information we consume is accurate.

College and Career Readiness Anchor Standards for Writing

Research to Build and Present Knowledge – Grade 8

- Conduct short as well as more sustained research projects based on focused questions, demonstrating understanding of the subject under investigation.

- Gather relevant information from multiple print and digital sources, assess the credibility and accuracy of each source, and integrate the information while avoiding plagiarism.

- Draw evidence from literary or informational texts to support analysis, reflection, and research.

Use Reinforcing Effort and Providing Recognition to enhance students' understanding of the relationship between effort and achievement by addressing students' attitudes and beliefs about learning. Provide students with rewards or praise for their accomplishments in creating and sharing with the community a presentation that compares the detail and timeliness of reporting of the same events in traditional media (print, television, radio).

D. exhibit leadership for digital citizenship.

Project task: Create a multimedia presentation that illustrates responsible research practices that students can use to avoid plagiarism.

New idea: *Framing the Problem, Finding the Fixes!* People realize that plagiarism is a problem, but don't agree on how big a problem it is or what to do about it. This aspect of the activity will provide the substance for your multimedia presentation. Contact professionals who work with these issues on a daily basis (both within and beyond education) to assess the magnitude of the problem. Investigate new products and services that have grown up to meet the demand of catching violators. Explore the information resources designed to instruct students and teachers on appropriate practices.

> ## College and Career Readiness Anchor Standards for Writing
>
> ### *Production and Distribution of Writing – Grade 8*
>
> - Produce clear and coherent writing in which the development, organization, and style are appropriate to task, purpose, and audience.
>
> - Develop and strengthen writing as needed by planning, revising, editing, rewriting, or trying a new approach.
>
> - Use technology, including the Internet, to produce and publish writing and to interact and collaborate with others.

Learning Strategies

Use Identifying Similarities and Differences to enhance students' understanding of and ability to use knowledge by engaging them in mental processes that involve identifying ways that appropriate research and plagiaristic practices are alike and different.

What Does NETS-S5 (Digital Citizenship) Challenge Students to Do in Math?

Students understand human, cultural, and societal issues related to technology and practice legal and ethical behavior. Students:

A. advocate and practice safe, legal, and responsible use of information and technology.

Project task: Read the Web page "How to Lie with Statistics" (http://faculty .washington.edu/chudler/stat3.html). Find examples of graphs and other data representations from the media to assess their truthfulness and ability to persuade or mislead a reader.

New idea: *Find the Flaws!* Discover what techniques are effective at twisting facts to fit a purpose and learn how to recognize when you're being fooled by statistics as presented in various media or student-created examples. Share findings with students, parents, and the community about how to distinguish between valid and suspect persuasive graphs and data.

Learning Strategies

Use Reinforcing Effort and Providing Recognition to enhance students' understanding of the relationship between effort and achievement by addressing students' attitudes and beliefs about learning. Provide students with rewards or praise for their accomplishments related to increasing data literacy.

B. exhibit a positive attitude toward using technology that supports collaboration, learning, and productivity.

Project task: Measure and compare the amount of time spent in school and at home doing homework, watching TV, playing video games, and communicating with friends (using cell phones, the Internet, and so on). Create graphical representations of data using graphing calculators and spreadsheets.

New idea: *Share and Compare!* Post your findings on a school website or wiki so that students and parents can get a sense of what a "day in the life" means to the students of today.

Learning Strategies

Use Reinforcing Effort and Providing Recognition to enhance students' understanding of the relationship between effort and achievement by addressing students' attitudes and beliefs about learning. Provide students with rewards or praise for their accomplishments in completing their study of how students spend their time in school and out of school.

C. demonstrate personal responsibility for lifelong learning.

Project task: Create a group portfolio that contrasts the choices available within a selected Career Cluster for people with well-developed mathematics and information,

> **Common Core State Standards – Math Grade 8**
>
> *Functions – 8.F*
>
> - Define, evaluate, and compare functions.
> - Use functions to model relationships between quantities.

communication, and technology (ICT) skills, and those without well-developed mathematics and ICT skills.

New idea: *Take Stock!* Career Clusters and Pathways describe the nature, requirements, and pay ranges for all existing jobs, many of which depend on well-developed mathematics and (ICT) skills. Take stock of what you are learning about potential careers that best align with your interests, preferences, and goals, and let this information guide choices about course selection, service learning, and extracurricular activities. What are all possible sources of information about Career Clusters and the role of mathematics and ICT skills in available choices and about trends for future impacts of technology in the workplace? Which are the best sources (accurate, authentic) that provide the information we need? How do we accurately summarize and cite the relevant information from the selected sources?

Learning Strategies

Use Identifying Similarities and Differences to enhance students' understanding of and ability to use knowledge by engaging them in mental processes that involve identifying ways that Career Pathways are alike and different. Use a variety of information resources to determine which Career Cluster is a student's most and least favorite in terms of providing direction for life after high school.

D. exhibit leadership for digital citizenship.

Project task: Join the Down the Drain project (http://www.ciese.org/curriculum/drainproj/). Use linked tables, graphs, and symbolic representations (as can be displayed in a spreadsheet) to explain how components of a real-world situation are connected and how changes could impact worldwide water use.

New idea: *Keep from Running Dry!* Even if the tap flows on demand now, the sustainability of any community hinges on having an adequate, sustainable source of fresh water. Using digital learning to help bring the issue to public awareness now is a crucial first step!

Learning
Strategies

Use Reinforcing Effort and Providing Recognition to enhance students' understanding of the relationship between effort and achievement by addressing students' attitudes and beliefs about learning. Provide students with rewards or praise for their accomplishments related to the attainment of a goal.

What Does NETS-S5 (Digital Citizenship) Challenge Students to Do in Science?

Students understand human, cultural, and societal issues related to technology and practice legal and ethical behavior. Students:

A. advocate and practice safe, legal, and responsible use of information and technology.

Project task: Design and implement a team science project that will address the factors that must be considered in making informed decisions about land use (for example, environmental impact, jobs, present and future values of natural resources). (Science Strand: science in personal and social perspectives)

New idea: *Share Findings Widely!* It is often said that "students are our future," but rarely are students viewed as designers of the future. Share the design of your model with professionals in the community who work on a daily basis with environmental impact, jobs, and present and future values of natural resources. Students' investigating growth trends and alerting adults for challenges on the horizon is real news. Share it!

Science Activity Type: Knowledge Expression

(Debate)

Students discuss opposing viewpoints embedded in science content knowledge, linked to ethics, nature of science, personal preferences, politics, etc.

Learning Strategies

Use Reinforcing Effort and Providing Recognition to enhance students' understanding of the relationship between effort and achievement by addressing students' attitudes and beliefs about learning. Provide students with rewards or praise for their accomplishments related to determining the factors that are involved in adequate planning for community growth.

B. exhibit a positive attitude toward using technology that supports collaboration, learning, and productivity.

Project task: Determine the change in the turbidity of a river after a rainfall and its effect on the plants and animals living in this habitat, by collecting real-time observations and searching print and electronic resources to gather and record past data for comparison. (Science Strand: Earth and space science)

New idea: *Connect with the Community!* In many communities, people who fish are the citizens most concerned about water quality. Presenting the findings from this activity can help raise awareness of the impact of land use on the condition of rivers and lakes.

Science Activity Type: Conceptual Knowledge Building

(Data Analysis)

Students describe relationships, understand cause-and-effect, prioritize evidence, determine possible sources of error/discrepancies, etc.

Learning Strategies

Use Reinforcing Effort and Providing Recognition to enhance students' understanding of the relationship between effort and achievement by addressing students' attitudes and beliefs about learning. Provide students with rewards or praise for their accomplishments in explaining the effects of rain on water turbidity and the consequences for plants and animals.

C. demonstrate personal responsibility for lifelong learning.

Project task: Maintain an online journal describing changes to a specific habitat over extended periods of time, and periodically evaluate entries to assess progress toward achieving the understanding of key ideas. (Science Strand: science in personal and social perspectives)

New idea: *Share Your Tips!* Gather the most successful habit-changing strategies and report them in the student school newspaper or in the PTA newsletter. If there are many, create a "tip of the month" feature in each issue.

Science Activity Type: Procedural Knowledge Building

(Observe, Do Procedures, Record Data)

- Students make observations from physical or digital experiences.

- Students run trials or otherwise carry out steps to investigations.

- Students record observational and recorded data in tables, graphs, images, lab notes.

Learning Strategies

Use Reinforcing Effort and Providing Recognition to enhance students' understanding of the relationship between effort and achievement by addressing students' attitudes and beliefs about learning. Provide students with rewards or praise for their accomplishments in evaluating and sharing their findings about changing habitats.

What Does NETS-S5 (Digital Citizenship) Challenge Students to Do in Geography?

Students understand human, cultural, and societal issues related to technology and practice legal and ethical behavior. Students:

A. advocate and practice safe, legal, and responsible use of information and technology.

Project task: Use the Internet to locate and download regional and global data about teenage purchase and sharing of recorded music, and prepare graphs comparing these two data sets for a multimedia presentation to the class.

New idea: *Do You Hear What I Hear?* Music defines teenage identity as much as clothing. But how does the music that students in your school listen to compare with the nation? How much of this music is purchased, downloaded, heard by broadcast, or shared? There are several ongoing global projects and groups (such as GlobalSchoolNet [http://www .globalschoolnet.org], YouthCaN [http://www.youthcanworld.org/], and ePals [http:// www.epals.com/]) that can help in connecting students around the world to determine what music teenagers in different parts of the world listen to and purchase. Analysis of data gathered from the Internet and from local and global student surveys can reveal trends. Challenge students to use visual imagery to express the meaning behind the numbers.

Geography Activity Type: Convergent Knowledge Expression

(Engage in Data-Based Inquiry)

Using student-generated data or print-based and digital data available online, students pursue original lines of inquiry.

Learning Strategies

Use Nonlinguistic Representation to enhance students' ability to represent and elaborate on knowledge using mental images. How can students use multiple data sources to prepare graphs comparing these two data sets for a multimedia presentation to the class?

B. exhibit a positive attitude toward using technology that supports collaboration, learning, and productivity.

Project task: Conduct visual analysis of remotely sensed images (aerial photographs and satellite imagery), using maps and other graphical representations of environmental data to determine other areas with environmental characteristics similar to yours, from local to global in scale, and present your findings for peer review.

New idea: *View from Above!* Reading about similarities between other areas and ours can't compare with seeing these similarities. Satellite and other aerial images provide us with information never before available. Organize teams to search each continent for areas that share environmental characteristics with ours. Organize images with supporting data that show similarities between areas. Organize an evening presentation of findings to a community group, to show which areas on earth share similar environmental characteristics to ours.

Geography Activity Type: Knowledge Building

(Compare/Contrast)

Students interrogate information to understand multiple characteristics, evidence, and/or perspectives on a topic.

Learning Strategies

Use Reinforcing Effort and Providing Recognition to enhance students' understanding of the relationship between effort and achievement by addressing students' attitudes and beliefs about learning. Provide students with rewards or praise for their accomplishments related to using remote imagery to identify other areas on earth that resemble theirs.

C. demonstrate personal responsibility for lifelong learning.

Project task: Challenge students to create a personal presentation that explains which geography-related Career Cluster is their most and least favorite in terms of providing direction for life after high school, using a variety of information resources.

New idea: *Learn How Geography Shows Up in Your Preferences!* Use the online Career Cluster Interest Survey (http://www.ctcd.edu/cc_survey/userdetail.aspx) to discover what Career Clusters and Pathways align with students' preferences and to guide investigations and research into the importance of well-developed geographical knowledge and skills to these potential choices. Compare what you are learning about potential careers that best align with your interests, preferences, and goals, and let this information guide choices about course selection, service learning, and extracurricular activities.

Geography Activity Type: Convergent Knowledge Expression

(Engage in Data-Based Inquiry)

Using student-generated data or print-based and digital data available online, students pursue original lines of inquiry.

Learning Strategies

Use Reinforcing Effort and Providing Recognition to enhance students' understanding of the relationship between effort and achievement by addressing students' attitudes and beliefs about learning. Provide students with rewards or praise for their accomplishments related to producing a compelling presentation about examining how personal interests align with geography-related Career Clusters and Pathways. Organize presentations for community groups and organizations for the most exemplary projects.

Recommended Activity: Project Speak Up

Speak Up, an annual national research project facilitated by Project Tomorrow, provides a powerful opportunity for students to exercise digital citizenship. The Speak Up data represent the largest collection of authentic, unfiltered stakeholder input on education, technology, 21st century skills, schools of the future, and science instruction. Through the lesson plans, students are introduced to the concept of contributing to local change and a national dialogue by voicing their opinions about their education. Project activities encourage students to reflect on their use of technology both in and out of school and on how they learn math, science, and 21st century skills. Education, business, and policy leaders report using the data regularly to inform federal, state, and local education programs.

Driving Questions

- How can students contribute to local change and a national dialogue by voicing their opinions about their education?

- How can students reflect on their use of technology both in and out of school and on how they learn math, science, and 21st century skills?

Purpose of the Speak Up Project

- Collect and report the unfiltered feedback from students, parents, and teachers on key educational issues.

- Use the data to stimulate local conversations.

- Raise national awareness about the importance of including the viewpoints of students, parents, and teachers in the education dialogue.

Any school, district, or organization that serves K–12 students may participate in Speak Up. All Speak Up participants become part of a growing movement that values and uses stakeholders' opinions to inform K–12 educational decisions. For more information, please visit http://www.tomorrow.org/speakup/.

Assessing Digital Citizenship (NETS-S5)

 Example: What student artifacts might prompt a student to say any of the following in a self-assessment?

- *I understand the rights, responsibilities, and limitations that come with creating and using both original work that I've produced and work created by others.*

- *I fully achieved the purpose of the task, including thoughtful, insightful interpretations and conjectures connecting the task to real-life applications.*

Technology Operations and Concepts (NETS-S6)

Technology Operations and Concepts make possible the digital communities of practice that support ongoing professional growth. When students and teachers discuss how use of the Internet, email, blogs, and forums have contributed to the experiences that have allowed them to learn, every one of this standard's elements comes into focus. Students have the opportunity to select from tools that include multimedia capabilities (such as PowerPoint presentations and streaming audio and video), calendars, surveys, and rich text editor capabilities, as well as searchable archives for easy access to past postings.

Students demonstrate a sound understanding of technology concepts, systems, and operations. Students:

A. understand and use technology systems.

B. select and use applications effectively and productively.

C. troubleshoot systems and applications.

D. transfer current knowledge to learning of new technologies.

What Does NETS-S6 (Technology Operations and Concepts) Challenge Students to Do in English?

Students demonstrate a sound understanding of technology concepts, systems, and operations. Students:

A. understand and use technology systems.

Project task: Given a variety of hyperlinked documents on a topic of personal interest, describe your own process for reading and evaluating a website or other text containing a variety of embedded links; share these reflections online and compare processes with classmates.

New idea: *Think, Then Link!* Students today have a variety of tools to connect them with ideas and resources. But do students know how these systems work, and when to choose one over another? Although everyone has a process for finding and dealing with information, most people don't examine the processes they use. Becoming aware of our current information-seeking strategies and how we might learn from the strategies of others is critical for lifelong learning.

College and Career Readiness Anchor Standards for Reading

Integration of Knowledge and Ideas (Reading Standards for Informational Text) – Grade 8

- Evaluate the advantages and disadvantages of using different mediums (e.g., print or digital text, video, multimedia) to present a particular topic or idea.

- Delineate and evaluate the argument and specific claims in a text, assessing whether the reasoning is sound and the evidence is relevant and sufficient; recognize when irrelevant evidence is introduced.

- Analyze a case in which two or more texts provide conflicting information on the same topic and identify where the texts disagree on matters of fact or interpretation.

Learning Strategies

Use Cues, Questions, and Advance Organizers to enhance students' ability to retrieve, use, and organize what they already know about hypertext links, search engines, websites, social bookmarking, and other technologies. Using such examples as a phonebook or yellow pages, "snail mail," and email, students can explain each new system in terms of how it is based on and extends the previous methods of linking information and people.

B. select and use applications effectively and productively.

Project task: Design a process to organize a project that develops and publishes a collaborative essay (a multiple-authored work) on a team-selected topic.

New idea: *Blueprint Your Skill Building!* Blueprints serve as a model for construction and allow us to measure progress against a plan. Rubrics for using research, collaboration, and publishing tools can help benchmark these skills as students progress through the activity. Keep track of which technology applications are considered and which are ultimately most useful (and why).

College and Career Readiness Anchor Standards for Writing

Production and Distribution of Writing – Grade 8

- Produce clear and coherent writing in which the development, organization, and style are appropriate to task, purpose, and audience.

- Develop and strengthen writing as needed by planning, revising, editing, rewriting, or trying a new approach.

- Use technology, including the Internet, to produce and publish writing and to interact and collaborate with others.

Learning Strategies

Use Setting Objectives and Providing Feedback to provide students a direction for learning and information about how well they are performing relative to using digital research and publishing tools, so that they can improve their performance.

C. troubleshoot systems and applications.

Project task: Using a digital video camera, record a "day in the life" montage of scenes from a classroom or the school as a whole, creating special effects with shooting angles, range, lighting, composition, and camera features. Describe the impact of these effects.

New idea: *Harvest Tips!* Video production uses every aspect of technology at one time or another. From drafting initial ideas for a script (word processing) to storyboarding (graphics and graphic organizers) and research (databases) to budgeting (spreadsheets) and background research (videoconferencing and audio recording), there are unlimited opportunities for troubleshooting the systems involved. Begin with an example "tip sheet" showing students how to construct a wiki to contain their guidance for using (and troubleshooting) new technologies. Provide feedback on the accuracy and thoroughness of their tips as they are developed.

College and Career Readiness Anchor Standards for Writing

Research to Build and Present Knowledge – Grade 8

- Conduct short as well as more sustained research projects based on focused questions, demonstrating understanding of the subject under investigation.

- Gather relevant information from multiple print and digital sources, assess the credibility and accuracy of each source, and integrate the information while avoiding plagiarism.

- Draw evidence from literary or informational texts to support analysis, reflection, and research.

Learning Strategies

Use Cues, Questions, and Advance Organizers to enhance students' ability to retrieve, use, and organize what they already know about technology systems they use at school and at home, and how their prior knowledge can help them strategize and troubleshoot when required.

D. transfer current knowledge to learning of new technologies.

Project task: Using a topic of interest (based on units covered in science, social studies, history, or math classes), create an annotated bibliography of important resource materials (books, newspapers, magazines, online sources, video, music, and so on). Include a working bibliography of sources consulted or skimmed but not selected.

New idea: *Go Beyond Index Cards!* Traditional ways of finding, evaluating, and organizing sources progress from handwritten notes to index cards to card catalogs, all the way to

College and Career Readiness Anchor Standards for Writing

Research to Build and Present Knowledge – Grade 8

- Conduct short as well as more sustained research projects based on focused questions, demonstrating understanding of the subject under investigation.

- Gather relevant information from multiple print and digital sources, assess the credibility and accuracy of each source, and integrate the information while avoiding plagiarism.

- Draw evidence from literary or informational texts to support analysis, reflection, and research.

sophisticated databases. Students need to learn which tools to use, as well as how and when to use them.

Learning
Strategies

Use Cues, Questions, and Advance Organizers to enhance students' ability to retrieve, use, and organize what they already know about finding and managing metadata (information about information) sources, in order to transfer this knowledge to current and future systems.

What Does NETS-S6 (Technology Operations and Concepts) Challenge Students to Do in Math?

Students demonstrate a sound understanding of technology concepts, systems, and operations. Students:

A. understand and use technology systems.

Project task: Create a group portfolio that contrasts the choices available within a selected Career Cluster for people with well-developed mathematics and information, communication, and technology (ICT) skills, and those without well-developed mathematics and ICT skills. (See http://www.careerclusters.org/ for more information.) (Math Strands: algebra, data analysis)

New idea: *What's a Career Pathway, Anyway?* Career Clusters and Pathways describe the nature, requirements, and pay ranges for all existing jobs, many of which depend on well-developed mathematics and (ICT) skills. Student exploration of Career Clusters through online databases and websites and through direct communication with industry professionals via email or audio- or videoconferencing provides multiple opportunities to learn the use of technology tools and processes. In addition, technology-based mathematical tools form a specific genre that greatly extends the powers of analysis and visualization available to individuals and groups.

Learning Strategies

Use Cues, Questions, and Advance Organizers to enhance students' ability to retrieve, use, and organize what they already know about a topic. Forecast the impact of technology changes for the Career Clusters students have identified as requiring the least well developed mathematics and ICT skills.

B. select and use applications effectively and productively.

Project task: Measure and compare the amount of time spent in school and at home doing homework, watching TV, playing video games, and communicating with friends (using cell phones, the Internet, and so on). Create graphical representations of data using graphing calculators, spreadsheets, and other data visualization tools. (Math Strand: data analysis)

New idea: *Make Time Visible!* Students need to know how to use the graphing capabilities of various programs to display accurate data representations of how students spend their time. Task students to keep track of which technology applications are considered and which are ultimately most useful (and why).

Common Core State Standards

Mathematical Practices (Grade 8)

1. Make sense of problems and persevere in solving them.

2. Reason abstractly and quantitatively.

3. Construct viable arguments and critique the reasoning of others.

4. Model with mathematics.

5. Use appropriate tools strategically.

Learning
Strategies

Use Setting Objectives and Providing Feedback to provide students a direction for learning and information about how well they are performing in visually communicating meaning from data so that they can improve their performance.

C. troubleshoot systems and applications.

Project task: Investigate whether local recycling efforts help conserve energy and natural resources and what proportion of the recycled materials are used in various items, by incorporating math concepts into a community service project. (Math Strand: data analysis)

New idea: *Use Mathematical Tools!* Digital technology allows for statistical analysis and data projections never before available to students. These tools are among the most sophisticated in existence, require intensive efforts to master, and offer ample opportunities for developing troubleshooting skills.

Learning
Strategies

Use Homework and Practice to extend the learning opportunities for students to practice, review, and apply knowledge. Enhance students' ability to reach the expected level of proficiency in the use of data analysis tools.

D. transfer current knowledge to learning of new technologies.

Project task: Determine the effects of an increasing student population on existing school bus capacity, routes, and schedules, using mathematical understanding and problem-solving processes to collaboratively identify problems. (Math Strands: algebra, data analysis)

> ## Common Core State Standards – Math Grade 8
>
> ### *Expressions and Equations – 8.EE*
>
> - Work with radicals and integer exponents.
> - Understand the connections between proportional relationships, lines, and linear equations.
> - Analyze and solve linear equations and pairs of simultaneous linear equations.

New idea: *Build Community!* Use online collaborative tools to conduct planning discussions. What tools and methods are most effective in getting input from people affected by changes in bus routes and schedules?

Learning
Strategies

Use Cues, Questions, and Advance Organizers to enhance students' ability to retrieve, use, and organize what they already know about finding and managing information about information sources, in order to transfer this knowledge to current and future systems.

What Does NETS-S6 (Technology Operations and Concepts) Challenge Students to Do in Science?

Students demonstrate a sound understanding of technology concepts, systems, and operations. Students:

A. understand and use technology systems.

Project task: Compile data gathered from sources to record and present results of local recycling efforts, using evidence collected from observations or other sources (for example, the Internet, databases, print materials) to create models and explanations. (Science Strand: science in personal and social perspectives)

New idea: *Then and Now!* Before recycling, unwanted "stuff" was simply dumped, out of sight, out of mind. Mass consumption habits in our society have resulted in many more times the amount of "stuff" being made, with fewer and fewer places to put it. Challenge students to use technology to create models to demonstrate the differences recycling has made and then to create a public service announcement (PSA) that includes quantifiable data showing the results of local recycling efforts and suggests ways to improve these results. Digital media tools make it possible for students to create high-quality video materials. How can students combine what they already know about computers, CD and DVDs, and effective videos?

Science Activity Type: Conceptual Knowledge Building

(Data Analysis)

Students describe relationships, understand cause-and-effect, prioritize evidence, determine possible sources of error/discrepancies, etc.

Learning
Strategies

Use Cues, Questions, and Advance Organizers to enhance students' ability to retrieve, use, and organize what they already know about PSAs.

B. select and use applications effectively and productively.

Project task: Investigate whether local recycling efforts help conserve energy and natural resources, using a broad range of tools and techniques to plan and conduct an inquiry to address the question. (Strand: Science in personal and social perspectives)

New idea: *Know the Right Tools for the Job!* This activity requires well-developed skills in information searching, data organizing and analysis, and presentation. A wide variety of tools exist for these purposes. Which are best for specific tasks, and which of these do students know how to use?

Learning Strategies

Use Setting Objectives and Providing Feedback to provide students a direction for learning and information about how well they are performing relative to using appropriate technology tools so that they can improve their performance.

C. troubleshoot systems and applications.

Project task: Design a multimedia presentation explaining the interrelationships of biotic and abiotic elements in a specific ecosystem, using a wide range of tools and a variety of oral, written, and graphic formats to share information and results of observations and investigations. (Science Strand: Earth and space science)

New idea: *Each One, Teach One!* Students' knowledge and skill levels with multimedia tools can vary greatly. Multimedia production uses every aspect of technology at one time or another. From drafting initial ideas for a script (word processing) to storyboarding (graphics and graphic organizers) and research (databases) to budgeting (spreadsheets) and background research (videoconferencing and audio recording), there are unlimited opportunities for troubleshooting the systems involved. Begin with an example "tip sheet" showing students how to construct a wiki to contain their guidance for using (and troubleshooting) new technologies. Provide feedback on the accuracy and thoroughness of their tips as they are developed.

Learning Strategies

Use Cooperative Learning to provide students with opportunities to interact with each other in groups in ways that enhance their learning. Harness what is known by providing a wiki for students to share their knowledge and identify areas for research, so that peers can fill in the gaps in their personal technology skills.

D. transfer current knowledge to learning of new technologies.

Project task: Identify factors to be considered in making informed decisions about land use and in deciding whether a new housing development will require building additional schools and, if necessary, where new schools should be built. (Science Strand: science in personal and social perspectives)

New idea: *Guided Practice!* Use online collaboration tools to help students master new tools, including geographic information systems (GISs), statistical analysis, and data visualization tools. Provide extended access to computers that have these tools as well as high-speed Internet connections.

Science Activity Type: Conceptual Knowledge Building

(Data Analysis)

Students describe relationships, understand cause-and-effect, prioritize evidence, determine possible sources of error/discrepancies, etc.

Learning
Strategies

Use Homework and Practice to extend the learning opportunities for students to practice, review, and apply knowledge. Enhance students' ability to reach the expected level of proficiency for a skill or process.

What Does NETS-S6 (Technology Operations and Concepts) Challenge Students to Do in Geography?

Students demonstrate a sound understanding of technology concepts, systems, and operations. Students:

A. *understand and use technology systems.*

Project task: Identify the best location for a new park according to defined criteria, using a geographic information system (GIS) to compare alternative sites.

New idea: *Learn Decision Tools!* Selecting the best location for new public facilities (such as new parks) depends on the outcomes of a number of "what ifs," including nearby population, easy access, topography, and others. GISs combine information in layers, each representing different aspects of a location. How were decisions about locating public facilities made in the past? What methods were used to gather information to support these decisions? What have these tools evolved into today?

Geography Activity Type: Convergent Knowledge Expression

(Engage in Data-Based Inquiry)

Using student-generated data or print-based and digital data available online, students pursue original lines of inquiry.

Learning
Strategies

Use Cues, Questions, and Advance Organizers to enhance students' ability to retrieve, use, and organize what they already know about using information to improve decision making.

B. select and use applications effectively and productively.

Project task: Collaborate with peers to create a series of Web pages that use maps to portray information about your hometown (for example, a community atlas).

New idea: *Map Your Community!* Challenge students to select the most interesting and relevant features of their hometown and then use Google Maps or Google Earth to generate images to create a community atlas. Students have varying degrees of technology knowledge and skills. As students begin using website building tools, have more experienced students compile "tip sheets" to orient the next group of students who will need to learn to use these tools.

Geography Activity Type: Knowledge Building

(Compare/Contrast)

Students interrogate information to understand multiple characteristics, evidence, and/or perspectives on a topic.

Learning
Strategies

Use Setting Objectives and Providing Feedback to provide students a direction for learning and information about how well they are performing relative to expanding their Web publishing skills so that they can improve their performance. Begin with an example "tip sheet" showing students how to construct a wiki to contain their guidance for new students. Provide feedback on the accuracy and thoroughness of their tips as they are developed.

C. troubleshoot systems and applications.

Project task: Conduct visual analysis of remotely sensed images (aerial photographs and satellite imagery), using maps and other graphical representations of environmental data to determine other areas with environmental characteristics similar to ours, from local to global in scale, and present findings for peer review.

New idea: *Use the GLOBE!* The Global Learning and Observations to Benefit the Environment (GLOBE) program is a worldwide hands-on, primary and secondary school–based science and education program. GLOBE's vision promotes and supports students, teachers, and scientists to collaborate on inquiry-based investigations of the environment and the Earth system working, in close partnership with NASA, NOAA, and NSF Earth System Science Projects (ESSPs) in study and research about the dynamics of Earth's environment.

Using World Wind (a 3-D earth-viewing application developed by NASA's Ames Research Center; http://viz.globe.gov/viz-bin/show.cgi?page=help-worldwind.ht) with GLOBE data provides a powerful way to visually compare environmental regions. Adding new systems to students' repertoire provides opportunities for strengthening and modeling trouble-shooting skills.

Use Homework and Practice to extend the learning opportunities for students to practice, review, and apply knowledge. Enhance students' ability to reach the expected level of proficiency for a skill or process. Provide opportunities for guided practice by creating student-narrated videos and using peer coaching.

Learning Strategies

D. *transfer current knowledge to learning of new technologies.*

Project task: Present an oral report on a recent major geographic event—hurricane, volcanic eruption, or earthquake—using different newspapers, news magazines, and Internet news sources.

New idea: *Invent to Save Lives!* Design an early warning system to alert populations in remote areas of impending danger from major geographic events. Animations and graphics can be more effective in communicating how saving minutes can save lives. The Internet makes nearly instantaneous information available globally, but the populations most at risk are least likely to have Internet connections or even electricity. How can these people be reached in time for early warnings to save lives? Important tasks, such as warning the general populace of impending danger, have always used the most advanced technologies available.

Science Activity Type: Conceptual Knowledge Building

(Data Analysis)

Students describe relationships, understand cause-and-effect, prioritize evidence, determine possible sources of error/discrepancies, etc.

Use Identifying Similarities and Differences to enhance students' understanding of and ability to use knowledge by engaging them in mental processes that involve identifying ways that warning systems are alike and different. Examine how methods have evolved over time to meet specific challenges using the technologies available at that point in history.

Learning Strategies

Leveraging Untapped Expertise: The GenYES Model

Research shows that students can be a highly effective part of the solution to many of the hurdles schools face as they strive to integrate technology into the curriculum. Although students make up approximately 92 percent of a school's population and are the "digital generation," they remain a largely untapped resource. I highly

---

recommend that you explore the Generation YES programs for developing both student and adult technology expertise in your school in conjunction with implementing the Digital Learning Process, because it is such a good fit. Literature review reveals decades of research which shows that leveraging and aligning peer mentoring, authentic assessment, PBL, and student voices are viable strategies in improving student learning.

Nationally, more than five hundred schools use the Generation YES programs GenYES (professional development) and TechYES (technology literacy) to prepare students to assist their own schools in meeting their technology goals. In one of GenYES's most powerful models, students who are members of Student Technology Leaders clubs provide two technology services to their school: (1) ensure that all students in the school are technology literate, and (2) provide assistance to faculty and staff as they integrate technology for improved student learning.

Eleven years of data collected by the Northwest Regional Educational Laboratory from the nationwide GenYES project indicate that "the program is an effective alternative for schools wishing to integrate technology into their regular curriculum and increase their use of project-based, student-centered learning practices. The model provides individualized support for educators who wish to increase their use of technology without becoming distracted from the essence of their jobs—building and delivering effective curriculum units and lesson plans."

More than fifty thousand teachers have received technology integration support from trained GenYES students. Surveys of these thousands of teachers reveal that they had overwhelmingly positive responses to the students' providing technology support and that they believed it had an impact on the way they would teach in the future.

The Generation YES program that deals with the Enhancing Education Through Technology (EETT) eighth-grade technology literacy mandate is called TechYES. TechYES also has generated an abundance of research showing the efficacy of students helping other students. Steven Schneider of the Woodside Research Consortium conducted the largest TechYES study in 2006. About five hundred eighth-grade students (peer mentors) were trained to support more than ten thousand seventh-grade students in forty-five high-needs California schools as they each created two projects to show they were technology literate. Pre- and post-test knowledge of the seventh graders showed at least a 500 percent increase in each of the areas of software, hardware, network, Net safety, and Web evaluation skills. All of the participating schools reported that "TechYES is a good way to ensure middle school student technology literacy." For more information about GenYES and TechYES, visit http://www.genyes.org/ and http://www.techyes.net.

Assessing Technology Operations and Concepts (NETS-S6)

Example: What would students say in response to either prompt?

> • *I use systematic processes to address technology problems I encounter (such as searching for and finding misplaced files on my computer, dealing with a "crashed" application, or reconnecting my computer to a wired or wireless network).*

• *I've developed and use strategies for continually updating my awareness of emerging technologies and their application to the learning process at all levels (student, family and community), using both technical and human and social networks.*

Chapter 6

Walking the Talk
Evolving Your Practice with NETS for Teachers

The premise of the teacher version of the National Educational Technology Standards (NETS-T) is clear: effective teachers model and apply the NETS-S as they design, implement, and assess learning experiences to engage students and improve learning; enrich professional practice; and provide positive models for students, colleagues, and the community. Here are the five standards for teachers:

NETS-T1: Facilitate and Inspire Student Learning and Creativity

NETS-T2: Design and Develop Digital-Age Learning Experiences and Assessments

NETS-T3: Model Digital-Age Work and Learning

NETS-T4: Promote and Model Digital Citizenship and Responsibility

NETS-T5: Engage in Professional Growth and Leadership

 It is necessary, but not sufficient, for us as teachers to develop the same skills as our students. The transformation we need in education requires far more than this. Examining the kinds of challenging, authentic, and supportive environments the Digital Learning Process employs to develop these skills can help us deepen our understanding of how we can reach these professional goals.

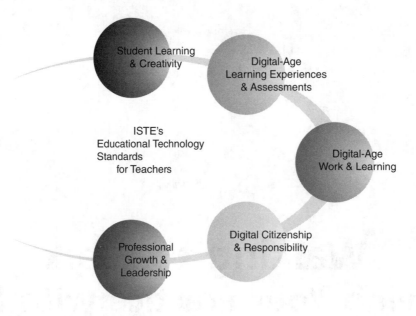

In this chapter, we'll explore the implications of each of the five standards and show how every Digital Learning Project provides you with opportunities to develop the required mastery.

As David Thornburg says, "If we are going to unlock the creativity of the students, we first have to unlock the creativity of the teachers."

What You Do with Technology Matters More Than Whether You Use It

We now have decades of research to draw on that was not available when technology was first introduced into classrooms. While debate has focused on student-to-computer ratios, the relative effectiveness of software programs, and impact on state test scores, it seems to me that we are missing the point if we reduce rich learning landscapes to flatland.

For those of you who are not familiar with the reference, *Flatland: A Romance of Many Dimensions* is a book written by E. A. Abbott in 1884, the rediscovery of which provokes delight in successive generations. (For the complete text, see http://www.ibiblio.org /eldritch/eaa/FL.HTM.)

The narrative is a thought experiment about how the world would seem to inhabitants aware of only two dimensions, instead of the three or four we take for granted. When we reduce educational landscapes to "basic skills versus higher-order thinking skills" or "direct instruction versus constructivism," we run the risk of returning to flatland.

Instead, as the figure suggests, we can examine where along the dimension of authenticity (from artificial to "real world") our use of technology appears. Examining our tools and practice quickly reveals that the majority of classroom technology use is aimed at a very low bar, and it is therefore not surprising that we don't see the larger gains that would come from aiming higher (and deeper).

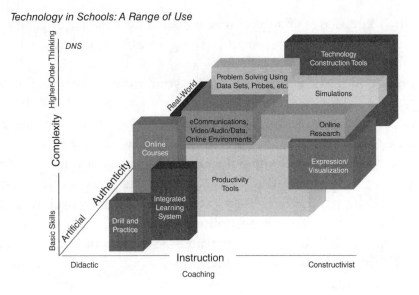

Technology in Schools: A Range of Use

In NETS-T, we must master not only everything students are required to do but also the interactions of complexity, instruction, and authenticity. It is important to remember that direct instruction is not inherently inferior to constructivism. The trick is knowing when to use each. This is where the "art" and "science" of teaching converge. NETS-T demand our fluency with all aspects of this work. However, the preponderance of work given to students gravitates toward the front left part of the matrix shown in the figure; this is why, in each Digital Learning Project, I'm working to build your confidence and the competence required to move you to the higher levels of practice.

NETS-T1: Facilitate and Inspire Student Learning and Creativity

Teachers use their knowledge of subject matter, teaching and learning, and technology to facilitate experiences that advance student learning, creativity, and innovation in both face-to-face and virtual environments.

Use the project ideas here to demonstrate your mastery of the following NETS-T indicators:

A. promote, support, and model creative and innovative thinking and inventiveness.

Welcome to the Global Village! What happens in one city ultimately impacts everyone. By investigating the relationships among political, social, and environmental change in cities in the developing world, you can help your students develop a good foundation of understanding to guide their actions and choices as adult digital citizens. Life in different cities is shaped by behaviors that depend on political, social, and environmental realities. For example, a city without adequate drinking water (environment) will make different decisions (political) about how that water will be used for agricultural, manufacturing, and residential activities (social) than will a city with ample water.

Driving question: What drives development in the developing world? Politics, social, and environmental factors play a role in every community. To understand their roles in the developing world, create challenges that prompt students to find out what role each factor plays in your community.

Document how you plan to use Identifying Similarities and Differences to enhance students' understanding of and ability to use knowledge by engaging them in mental processes that involve identifying ways that political, social, and environmental issues are alike and different. Use websites like CityMayors (http://www.citymayors.com/index.html) to get a profile of the complex issues facing the leaders of the cities of the world, to guide student collaboration and research strategies.

Learning Strategies

B. engage students in exploring real-world issues and solving authentic problems using digital tools and resources.

Invent to Save Lives! Challenge your students to design an early warning system to alert populations in remote areas of impending danger from major geographic events, based on a recent event—hurricane, volcanic eruption, or earthquake—using different newspapers, news magazines, and Internet news sources.

Driving question: Important tasks, like warning the general populace of impending danger, have always used the most advanced technologies available. The Internet makes nearly instantaneous information available globally, but the populations most at risk are least likely to have Internet connections or even electricity. How can these people be reached in time for early warnings to save lives?

Document how you plan to use Cues, Questions, and Advance Organizers to enhance your students' ability to retrieve, use, and organize what they already know about the need for early warning systems for natural disasters. Document

Learning Strategies

how you plan to use Identifying Similarities and Differences to enhance students' understanding of and ability to use knowledge by engaging them in mental processes that involve identifying ways that warning systems are alike and different. Examine how methods have evolved over time to meet specific challenges using the technologies available at that point in history.

C. promote student reflection using collaborative tools to reveal and clarify students' conceptual understanding and thinking, planning, and creative processes.

Predict the Future? Invent it! Most of the careers in which students will work have not yet been invented. How do they prepare for that? By making sure they learn how to learn. Develop a reflective online journal or blog detailing new understandings, connections, and ideas developing in the course of creating an individual capstone project on the personal impact of 21st century skills.

Use Cooperative Learning to provide students with opportunities to interact with each other in groups in ways that enhance their learning. Team assistance for individual projects is a good collaborative strategy for this activity. Each individual will have a personal capstone, but students vary in their skills as researchers, writers, and artists, and can assist one another by sharing their strengths.

D. model collaborative knowledge construction by engaging in learning with students, colleagues, and others in face-to-face and virtual environments.

Collaborate Globally! Partner up with classes from other cultures, through the free projects provided by ePals (http://www.epals.com/). For example, investigate Traditional Mythology or The Way We Are.

Driving question: How does writing become "timeless"?

Document how you plan to use Cooperative Learning to provide students with opportunities to interact with each other in groups in ways that enhance their learning. Collaborate with email pals and online mentors from other cultures and geographical areas in order to write a collaborative essay or create an interactive, interpretive project. Use a "real time" conferencing system (such as Skype or iChat) to conduct interviews of one student authoring team by another. Schedule each according to the time zone needs of the remote audience, and hold the event where community attendance is easiest.

How would you assess yourself? Respond to any prompt:

Example 1: Presentation—creativity. My presentations include language, features, and information that surprise readers and communicate my themes.

Example 2: Task analysis—making connections. I go beyond the requirements of the problem and find a relationship, connection, or extension to a new situation or concept in the content area I'm teaching.

Example 3: Critical thinking—making inferences. I use my own experiences, knowledge of the content and conventions, and tools of the subject matter to make inferences about new information I am learning as a teacher.

NETS-T2: Design and Develop Digital-Age Learning Experiences and Assessments

Teachers design, develop, and evaluate authentic learning experiences and assessments incorporating contemporary tools and resources to maximize content learning in context and to develop the knowledge, skills, and attitudes identified in the NETS-S.

Use the project ideas here to demonstrate your mastery of the following NETS-T indicators:

A. design or adapt relevant learning experiences that incorporate digital tools and resources to promote student learning and creativity.

Pick any of the four previous project ideas *(Welcome to the Global Village; Invent to Save Lives! Predict the Future? Invent it!* or *Collaborate Globally!)* and identify the digital tools and resources you'll use in implementing the project. What strategies will you use to increase the authenticity and complexity dimensions of the work students will perform?

B. develop technology-enriched learning environments that enable all students to pursue their individual curiosities and become active participants in setting their own educational goals, managing their own learning, and assessing their own progress.

Using the project you selected, develop a strategy to gradually move students from relying on your direct instruction to higher levels of independence and then teamwork. How can you accelerate this transition through the use of communication and collaboration tools you've learned about previously in this book? What role might wikis, blogs, or other online learning tools play in helping you guide students to take greater ownership of the process?

C. customize and personalize learning activities to address students' diverse learning styles, working strategies, and abilities using digital tools and resources.

How does your understanding of universal design for learning increase your ability to identify and respond to students' needs for multiple means of expression, representation, and engagement? Take inventory of your current preferred modalities, select one group of students who would benefit from your adding at least one new "channel" to use with them, and record your success in adding new techniques to your repertoire.

D. provide students with multiple and varied formative and summative assessments aligned with content and technology standards and use resulting data to inform learning and teaching.

Use the Digital Learning Trends spreadsheet to organize data from the formative assessments (observations) you glean in implementing two projects over the course of a semester or year. This will allow you to see trends for students and classes and to identify areas where you are already successful and where you've increased your success by focusing on areas where students may be struggling. Keep a journal so that you can build both a personal tool kit as well as compile information you can share with your colleagues.

Authentic experiences foster intrinsic motivation and engagement in learning. This standard acknowledges that such experiences are not likely to happen by accident, and require highly skilled teachers at the helm. Where can you go to develop such skills and see best practices modeled? Finding the right partners and well-designed projects is not a trivial task!

Effective communication, across all 21st century media, goes far beyond spelling and grammar in reports for other subjects. All currently used standards-based assessments include open-ended writing prompts, designed to demonstrate the reasoning behind students' approaches to solving problems, along with the solutions they submit. Comprehension in identifying the tasks posed by assessment questions, as well as clarity of written expression used in the responses, are both key skills students must develop to improve their performance.

It's important to remember that everything done on a computer is not necessarily a digital age learning experience. One could take a hand-drawn sketch, scan it into a computer, and then print it out. Or one could simply use a photocopier. Same goal, same process, different tools, same result. In the 1960s, students completed Iowa tests filling in bubble sheets with no. 2 pencils. Taking the same test on a computer is about as 21st century as making a photocopy.

The researchers at SEIR-TEC have an interesting point of view on this topic. They remind us,

Don't forget that traditional methods of assessment seldom measure the things that technology supports best, such as critical thinking, problem solving, creativity, design, productivity, and communication. We have found that one of the best ways to measure different kinds of achievement is through authentic assessments, such as products of learning and portfolios of students' work. In addition to providing real examples of what students are capable of doing, portfolios help students learn how to judge their own work and identify potential areas for growth. We realize that in this era of high-stakes testing, test scores are often the bottom line, but we have found that many policymakers and funding agencies are willing to take a broader view of achievement as long as there is solid evidence that students are learning what they're supposed to learn.[1]

Insights on 21st Century Assessment from Tina Rooks

The following material is from transcripts of a video interview with Tina Rooks. Tina has been a primary contributor to Turning Technologies' school improvement initiative for K–12. She has over sixteen years' experience in education, as a classroom teacher, middle school principal, technology administrator, and vice president of the professional development division of an educational technology company. Clips from this video interview are also available on the DVD that accompanies this book.

I think it's critical to develop effective formative assessments as we move down a path where we are going to integrate more and more technology into the classroom, yet oftentimes those technologies are not directly linked to a standard or have a nice pretty packaged assessment to go with it. And sometimes it's scary as we go down this path, because the expectation, particularly by No Child Left Behind, good, bad, or otherwise, is that we need to see progress and we need to monitor that progress. And that's just good teaching practice regardless of whether it's mandated or not.

So as we move down the path of using the newer technologies or going into project-based learning, having a mechanism to constantly progress-monitor students is really critical, and that kind of developed my love of student response systems and using that a variety of ways.

But I quickly learned that if we did not have appropriate questions, at appropriate times in the learning process, then it was somewhat meaningless. And so I've really worked with teachers in terms of some of the innovative things I want to bring in the classroom and then pairing that with some really meaningful assessment, assessment for learning, which has become kind of a buzzword, as we all know, but it's the just-in-time assessment as well. And I often call it 21st century assessment; it may not be a modeled assessment that we were used to seeing in the past. But it's assessment embedded in instruction and giving us a reflection on a daily basis.

Are our kids understanding? Are they growing with these concepts, and are we seeing the type of progress that we want to see? If we are not, then what am I going to do about it in the moment? How can I be that agile teacher? I think that lends itself really well to the different technology tools in the classroom, but it also can be somewhat of an art that you do have to kind of start practicing for an assessment model.

Self-concept (In Charge of Your Own Learning)

We are not going to reach every child simply by luck. Given that currently one-third of U.S. students don't graduate high school, clearly there are many millions of students for whom the traditional "stand and deliver" teacher lecturing from the front of the classroom can't be the only answer we provide. This means tailoring both our instruction and our assessments to meet the needs of all learners, harnessing and leveraging the full potential of digital technologies to individualize and personalize the content, environment, and experiences of learning.

How would you assess yourself? Respond to any prompt:

Example 1: Modeling universal design for learning—representation. I consider the diverse characteristics of my students and provide multiple means of representation, to give learners various ways of acquiring information and knowledge.

Example 2: Modeling universal design for learning—expression. I consider the diverse characteristics of my students and provide multiple means of expression, to provide learners alternatives for demonstrating what they know.

Example 3: Modeling universal design for learning—engagement. I consider the diverse characteristics of my students and provide multiple means of engagement, to tap into learners' interests, offer appropriate challenges, and increase motivation.

NETS-T3: Model Digital-Age Work and Learning

Teachers exhibit knowledge, skills, and work processes representative of an innovative professional in a global and digital society.

Use the following project ideas to demonstrate your mastery of the following NETS-T indicators:

A. demonstrate fluency in the use of technology systems and the transfer of current knowledge to new technologies and situations.

Begin with the project you selected from NETS-T1 *(Welcome to the Global Village! Invent to Save Lives! Predict the Future? Invent It!* or *Collaborate Globally!)*. What technology systems that you're already comfortable with and confident in using did you select? What new systems did you begin to incorporate into your activities? How did your prior knowledge provide a bridge to these new technologies? Most important, who helped you, and how did they help you make these connections? Whom in turn did you help to master technologies you already know but that were a challenge for them?

B. collaborate with students, peers, parents, and community members using digital tools and resources to support student success and innovation.

In our model of cascading mentorship, everyone is simultaneously a learner and a mentor. Which situations placed you in the learner role? Who served as your mentor in these situations, and what was the experience like? How were relationships affected (strengthened? altered?) by having you, as teacher, appear in an unexpected role? How would you answer these same questions when you were in the mentorship role (with peers, parents, or community)?

C. communicate relevant information and ideas effectively to students, parents, and peers using a variety of digital-age media and formats.

What worked best as you communicated and collaborated with students, parents, and peers? Capture both the techniques you used to promote engagement as well as the tools that worked best for you. For example, it has been suggested that teenagers will not use websites but will almost exclusively use text messaging. Did you find this to be the case?

D. model and facilitate effective use of current and emerging digital tools to locate, analyze, evaluate, and use information resources to support research and learning.

Using the Digital Learning Trends spreadsheet as a starting point, what other data analysis tools does your district provide (these may be part of the district student information system, a statewide accountability system, or longitudinal data system)? What supports are you and your peers provided in becoming "data fluent" in using information about student performance to inform and shape your instructional practice?

Learning is both a socially shared and individually constructed enterprise. This standard applies the power of "networked knowing." Classrooms may be the last remaining venue for the "sage on the stage," as almost every other domain in society has moved to a more socially constructed source for the knowledge that fuels growth. By encouraging teachers to bring contemporary work and learning practices within the classroom walls, teachers open possibilities to strengthen learning in even more powerful ways, applying another digital age lesson: learning with another person, especially an adult, is deeply motivating and inspires individuals to reach further for understanding.

Margaret Riel observes,

Our models are shifting. You can see it in our TV programs. Perry Mason has been replaced by a CSI team. Dr. Kildare has been replaced by *Grey's Anatomy.* The Superman superheroes have been replaced by Ninja Turtles who work in a group. These are cross-generational—both genders, multiracial groups that work together with mentors and novices, and people with different talents bringing together their skills. That's the way our society is going. But our schools really haven't gone that way yet.

It's one thing to say, classrooms should change. But until we change the position of teachers, classrooms aren't going to change because as long as the teacher is the sole person teaching a group of kids, then you're going to have a sense that it's that Superman, Dr. Kildare, or Perry Mason running the show, and what you really need is groups of teachers teaching groups of students. And when that happens we will see real change in schools.

We can start that now, and that's what Learning Circles really attempts to do: to get teachers to see the power of working in groups as opposed to working alone. When they sense that power, then it's easy for them to create that situation for their students. It just happens naturally because they understand what it's like.

 How would you assess yourself? Respond to any prompt:

Example 1: Problem solving—reflection. I reflect on my problem-solving processes, evaluate how well they are working, and make changes when necessary, to become more efficient, accurate, collaborative, and creative.

Example 2: Modeling teamwork—managing my own learning. I take a thoughtful, active role in my own learning. I challenge myself on a daily basis so that I can contribute my best to the group. I consistently demonstrate an honest desire to learn and share my ideas with my team.

Example 3: Modeling collaboration—metacognition. I ask the group to consider how well we are working together. I initiate discussions, ask important questions, act as a leader in the group, and help the group work together better.

Digital Learning

NETS-T4: Promote and Model Digital Citizenship and Responsibility

Teachers understand local and global societal issues and responsibilities in an evolving digital culture and exhibit legal and ethical behavior in their professional practices.

This standard is different from the others, because it hinges on your intention. Any single project can be implemented so that it exclusively focuses on academic goals or so that it simultaneously "makes a difference in the real world" in the process of meeting academic goals. The difference depends on why and how your students implement the project. Use the discussion here to prompt your thinking about how you will demonstrate mastery of the following NETS-T indicators:

A. advocate, model, and teach safe, legal, and ethical use of digital information and technology, including respect for copyright, intellectual property, and the appropriate documentation of sources.

When you use digital resources, do you make sure to appropriately cite sources? Do you have students explain their understanding of what is "fair use" and when the boundary to unethical or illegal use is being crossed? How do you approach issues of cyber-bullying? These real-world concerns offer opportunities for students to develop informed understandings of the realities of life in a digital world.

B. address the diverse needs of all learners by using learner-centered strategies and providing equitable access to appropriate digital tools and resources.

In the early days of Internet use, the puzzling lack of assignments that leveraged the power of digital resources could be traced back to the desire of school districts to avoid lawsuits. It was feared that once mandatory assignments were given that required Internet use, parents would soon line up suing the district to provide computers and Internet access if they could not afford it themselves. Although as teachers we can't singlehandedly take on the digital divide, we can support community efforts to expand access, by demonstrating the improved learning that results from effective use.

C. promote and model digital etiquette and responsible social interactions related to the use of technology and information.

Simply stated, we must walk the talk, reflectively and consciously, so that we can share the reasons for our actions and decisions.

D. develop and model cultural understanding and global awareness by engaging with colleagues and students of other cultures using digital age communication and collaboration tools.

It is vital that we select from (and engage with) the numerous options we have for global collaboration.

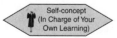 How would you assess yourself? Respond to any prompt:

Example 1: Ethics—fair use. I understand the rights, responsibilities, and limitations that come with creating and using both original work that I've produced as well as using work created by others.

Example 2: Digital equity. I know the difference between equality (everyone gets the same) and equity (everyone gets what he or she needs) and can make sound recommendations for appropriate digital tools and resources that can strengthen learning for the students who need them.

Example 3: Learner profiles. I know and use strategies to identify the learner profiles for each of my students. I can help them learn to use their strengths to bypass their weaknesses.

NETS-T5: Engage in Professional Growth and Leadership

Teachers continuously improve their professional practice, model lifelong learning, and exhibit leadership in their school and professional community by promoting and demonstrating the effective use of digital tools and resources.

Use the discussion here to prompt your thinking about how you will demonstrate your mastery of the following NETS-T indicators:

A. participate in local and global learning communities to explore creative applications of technology to improve student learning.

B. exhibit leadership by demonstrating a vision of technology infusion, participating in shared decision making and community building, and developing the leadership and technology skills of others.

C. evaluate and reflect on current research and professional practice on a regular basis to make effective use of existing and emerging digital tools and resources in support of student learning.

D. contribute to the effectiveness, vitality, and self-renewal of the teaching profession and of their school and community.

At this point, we will return to the observations of Margaret Riel, who has developed key recommendations for professional leadership and growth, as discovered through her thirty years of work in developing the Learning Circles model.

Until we get teachers and researchers working in concert and continuously, researchers serving teachers and teachers participating and being an active part of the development of knowledge, we are not going to have the kind of profession that will really move us forward. But we have everything in place now: we have TeacherTube so that teachers can create video artifacts of their classroom, which may be much easier for them than writing papers.

There are some great Internet resources. I'm thinking of the Inquiry Learning Forums that we've done in Indiana, where teachers put whole lessons on and then they describe their lessons and they actually reflect on their lessons so you can see the difference between a description and a reflection, and then they provide all the artifacts, and open up a dialogue around, was this a good example of teaching or could we address this problem in a different way than what I did in the classroom? That kind of lesson study is what will move the field forward in a way that is very powerful.

So I see the technology in two ways: both what can be done with it in the classroom, and I think that's what most people focus on, but it's also a terrific tool for including teachers in a learning environment, which I think is missing in schools and in a leadership environment, both of those two are critical.

You! Yes, you with the book in your hand! You're a leader! Don't try wiggling out of it: every project needs a leader, and you're it!

Communication and collaboration are both fundamental factors that mobilize people to act, as well as strategies that successful leaders employ to bring about action. These skills have always been valued, but they take on even more significance in the digital age. Just as teachers need to create curricula that meet standards, whether working for their own classrooms or as collaborative efforts with other teachers and schools, the need for project support permeates any educational institution.

Mentorship is the key, whether for our students (in working with professionals whose "day job" is what we're studying in class), or ourselves (in working with colleagues who are creating better methods and opportunities for learning our craft). There's research to support this approach as well: this chart, adapted from Joyce and Showers, demonstrates the changes in classroom practice that can result when we help one another through coaching and mentoring:[2]

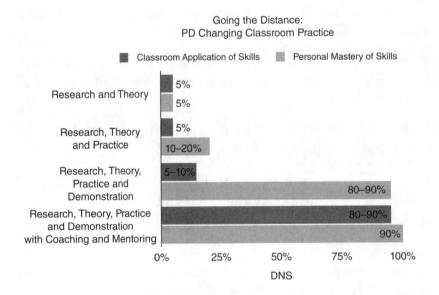

In many circles, professional Development (PD) is a topic that has baggage, because it is perceived as ineffective, time-consuming, expensive, and lacking in relevance. This chart helps us understand why people might draw such conclusions. If PD limits its focus to the transmission of information (research and theory) we see only 5 percent levels of personal mastery or classroom application.

The chart suggests that as we add different components to the PD experience, we can achieve increased levels of personal mastery (a good thing!), but we don't necessarily see a corresponding change in classroom practice. Hence the conclusion that very often PD doesn't "move the needle" for student achievement.

When we apply research, theory demonstrations, and practice in a collaborative context that explicitly expects more experienced people to assist people who are new to these practices, you can see pretty easily which approach is going to build a bridge between personal mastery and classroom practice.

Digital Learning

As enthusiastic as I am about having provided you all of the preceding information and suggestions, and as hopeful as I am that you are experiencing enthusiasm as well, here is fair warning: any attempts at positive change in established systems will encounter resistance directly proportional to the intensity of change being pursued. It can be helpful to consider the nature of obstacles you are likely to face so that you can be better prepared to deal with them.

Among the obstacles facing leaders (according to Warren Bennis, noted author and founding chairman of USC's Leadership Institute) are

- An information glut

- Factions that make consensus increasingly difficult

- Loss of community and civility

- Alterations in the nature of work and the economy

In facing these obstacles, and others that are peculiar to the world of education, it is more important than ever that we seek out, nurture, and sustain communities of practice. Once you start walking down the path of PBL, you are not likely to willingly turn back. The educational rewards are simply too great to ignore. Here again, we encounter a difference that digital age learning can introduce to the equation. Even if such challenges keep you up at night, right now, at this very moment, somewhere on this planet, there is another educator who is awake, thinking about the same issues you are, and most likely online to boot!

 How would you assess yourself? Respond to any prompt:

Example 1: Professional learning networks—strategies. I've developed and use a personal set of strategies for learning about, investigating, and joining available local and global learning communities appropriate to my needs and resources.

Example 2: Discussion—engagement. I enjoy class discussions because I learn from hearing other people's points of view. I connect what other people say to my own experiences and opinions. I draw conclusions about the topic being discussed.

Example 3: Problem solving—open-ended tasks. I continue to work enthusiastically on meaningful problems, even when I know that they may not have simple, correct answers.

Appendix A

Connect Your Classroom and Real Life
Career Clusters

? Need to Know
(Why You Do)

The answers for digital learning are not in the back of the book (not in any book, in fact). Instead, the questions provide us a way to successfully connect what we ask students to do in our classrooms and what life will ask them to do when they leave us. In this appendix, we address the vital ways in which 21st century success depends on highly developed academic skills, but seen from the viewpoint of 21st century employment. In the next decade, 80 percent of job growth will be in knowledge management and creation.

Employers' View of Skill Levels and High School Students

The gap between the skills employers rank as "very important" and the skills they see in high school graduates they consider for employment is significant.

Fortunately, these are precisely the skills students develop and strengthen by completing Digital Learning Projects. The set of four projects we'll examine in this appendix is specifically tailored to identify the connections between academic subject areas and 21st century skills, by exploring how these skills are applied in the Career Clusters and Pathways.

Skill	Percentage of Employers Rating High School Graduates as "Deficient"	Percentage of Employers Ranking This Skill as "Very Important"
Written communications (business writing)	80.9	52.7
Professionalism and work ethic	70.3	80.3
Writing in English (including grammar and spelling)	72.0	49.4
Critical thinking and problem solving	69.6	57.5
Mathematics	53.5	30.4
Reading comprehension	38.4	62.5

Source: Are They Really Ready to Work? by Jill Casner-Lotto and Mary Wright Benner, 2006, USA: Conference Board, Corporate Voices for Working Families, the Partnership for 21st Century Skills, Society for Human Resource Management. http://www.p21.org/documents/FINAL_REPORT_PDF09-29-06.pdf.

Career Clusters are groupings of occupations used as an organizing tool for curriculum design. Instruction in a Career Cluster prepares learners for a full range of career opportunities within that cluster, focusing on critical knowledge and skills that are transferable as new opportunities arise and the industry changes. Nationally, sixteen Career Clusters are recognized, with seventy-nine Career Pathways identified. This collection of Career Clusters and Pathways presents a way to categorize thousands of occupations currently available. For more information about Career Clusters, visit http://www.careerclusters.org. For a detailed case study of how an innovative school district (Ft. Sumner, New Mexico) implemented a successful strategy based on the Marketing Career Cluster, see http://www.careerclusters.org/resources/coolideas/Fort_Sumner_Guide_final_web_version.pdf.

Let's learn how to implement a Career Clusters or multidisciplinary project for your students that includes a series of learning experiences. Using what we learned earlier about TPACK activity types, we'll explore how the activities align with each of the six NETS (Creativity and Innovation; Communication and Collaboration; Research and Information Fluency; Critical Thinking, Problem Solving, and Decision Making; Digital Citizenship; and Technology Operations and Applications). As you select and combine these activities to best meet the needs of your particular students, be sure that there are one or more activity types for each standard. Also be sure to keep in mind how the project is an authentic 21st century project, meaning one that connects academics with real life, through digital learning.

How 21st Century Careers Depend on Highly Developed Core Subject Skills

Career Clusters projects share a common task statement: use a variety of information resources to determine which Career Cluster is a student's most and least favorite in terms of providing direction for life after high school.

Many of us grew up and were educated in a time when there was a sharp division between those students who were being prepared to go to college and everyone else, who were being prepared for "blue collar" (noncollege) employment, sometimes called vocational-technical or Vo-Tech. Unfortunately, this created a stigma that persists and obscures the changing nature of work in the digital age. Today, all students need to be College and Career Ready, and the rising tide of complexity demands performance levels of all workers that used to be reserved for those going to college. In fact, the truth is that "middle-skill" jobs, which require more than a high school education but not a four-year degree, currently make up the largest segment of jobs in the U.S. economy and will continue to do so for many years to come. In short, everyone needs to examine the career paths that open up according to educational attainment and to make informed decisions about his or her course of study on that basis.

As described on the Career Clusters website, "Career clusters link what students learn in school with the knowledge and skills they need for success in college and careers. Career clusters identify pathways from secondary school to two- and four-year colleges, graduate school, and the workplace, so students can learn in school what they can do in the future. This connection to future goals motivates students to work harder and enroll in more rigorous courses."

In the following Digital Learning Project, students use the online Career Cluster Interest Survey (http://www.ctcd.edu/cc_survey/userdetail.aspx) to discover what Career Clusters and Pathways align with the students' preferences, to guide investigations and research. Students first complete a profile by visiting this website, which provides survey results that suggest to them the top three Career Clusters that match their interest profile. Students then do Internet research to learn more about the career pathways in these clusters and work in teams to determine which holds the greatest (and least) interest for each student. The DVD contains screencasts of the survey and sample activities you can use to launch your students on their investigations. For more information, visit http://www.careerclusters.org/.

English/Language Arts—It's Everywhere (Even Your Future!)

In the 21st century, literacy takes on an expanded definition, one in which everyone must function as reader, author, editor, researcher, publisher, and information professional at one time or another. Communications can take on more forms than ever before, and students must become fluent in each one. Moreover, the comprehension and creative aspects of locating, interacting with, and applying information in all forms are entry-level expectations of 21st century employers.

No one knows for sure what he or she will end up doing for a job, especially today's students. It's predicted that they'll work in up to five different career fields, three of which have not yet even been invented. However, all jobs, old and new, share certain aspects in the nature of their work, and that is what Career Clusters are all about. Comparing "likes and dislikes" with the characteristics of each Career Cluster is a good way to get students started in charting their path right now! As a writing task, students can respond to these prompts:

- *Blacksmiths, wheelwrights, and scriveners.* How would these "workers of yesteryear" have forecast the impact that technology changes would have for their careers?

- *Tell me again, why should I care?* Many parents and students adopt a *que sera, sera* mentality toward examining potential career choices before graduation, saying "It's far too early to know what you're going to do for the rest of your life."

However, whether a student is interested in being an astronaut, a veterinarian, a lawyer, or a builder, there are certain courses he or she will need to take before graduating high school. The choices students make now have consequences in terms of either opening or closing doors to options they will want to have later. Students can always change their minds later (especially when a new career they like better is invented!), but it is much harder to return to high school to "redo" a set of choices when the consequences become obvious too late.

Math—How Will I Ever Use This in Real Life?

Mathematics has been called the universal language of science. It is also known as the gatekeeper for advancing to higher education and the expanded opportunities that result. Students' trouble with math often stems from difficulty in identifying the information-based tasks of the problem and understanding which mathematical processes are needed for the solutions. The comprehension and synthesis aspects of locating, interacting with, and applying information in all forms are entry-level expectations of 21st century employers.

Create a group portfolio that contrasts the choices available within any selected Career Cluster for people with well-developed mathematics and information, communication, and technology (ICT) skills and for those without well-developed mathematics and ICT skills.

Science—It's Everywhere (Even Your Future!)

Beyond the obvious links to STEM careers, science skills show up in all sixteen Career Clusters. The ability to apply the skills of reading, writing, reasoning, and speaking is central to meaningful participation in making societal decisions that depend on scientific understanding.

In the 21st century, science has moved out of the lab and into every aspect of our lives. Understanding the impact of decisions about how we live upon the systems that sustain life on this planet becomes increasingly important every day. We seek to move from habit and opinion as a basis of explaining observable phenomena to systems of continually evolving understandings emerging from the scientific method. Which careers seem most exciting or "cool" to students? Is there any relationship between the degree of "coolness" and links to science?

Geography: It's Everywhere (Even Your Future!)

Although geography too seldom appears in conversations about core subjects and accountability, it provides a meeting place for the application of language arts, math, and science. Application of these core subjects outside their traditional classrooms and high-stakes assessments has been shown to be a more effective strategy for strengthening higher-order thinking and problem-solving skills than simply "teaching to the test."

Learning Strategies

The interactions between human activity and the physical world we live in show up in all sixteen Career Clusters. Use Identifying Similarities and Differences to enhance students' understanding of and ability to use knowledge by engaging them in mental processes that involve identifying the ways that geographical issues that appear in various Career Clusters and pathways are alike and different.

Challenge each student to create a personal presentation that explains which geography-related Career Cluster is her or his most and least favorite, in terms of providing direction for life after high school, using a variety of information resources.

Creativity & Innovation

D. identify trends and forecast possibilities.

Students will complete the Career Cluster Interest Survey and, using that information, review online and print resources relating to the suggested areas of interest. In doing so, they will have the opportunity to demonstrate application of the following skills:

> ## College and Career Readiness Anchor Standards for Writing
>
> ### *Research to Build and Present Knowledge – Grade 8*
>
> • Conduct short as well as more sustained research projects based on focused questions, demonstrating understanding of the subject under investigation.
>
> • Gather relevant information from multiple print and digital sources, assess the credibility and accuracy of each source, and integrate the information while avoiding plagiarism.
>
> • Draw evidence from literary or informational texts to support analysis, reflection, and research.

A. interact, collaborate, and publish with peers, experts, or others employing a variety of digital environments and media.

Students will research potential interviewees from their identified fields of interest, as well as relevant websites that provide greater clarity about the realities of working in these fields. In doing so, they will have the opportunity to demonstrate application of the following skills:

College and Career Readiness Anchor Standards for Writing

Production and Distribution of Writing – Grade 8

- Produce clear and coherent writing in which the development, organization, and style are appropriate to task, purpose, and audience.

- Develop and strengthen writing as needed by planning, revising, editing, rewriting, or trying a new approach.

- Use technology, including the Internet, to produce and publish writing and to interact and collaborate with others.

B. locate, organize, analyze, evaluate, synthesize, and ethically use information from a variety of sources and media.

New idea: *Learn Your Preferences!* Using results from the online Career Cluster Interest Survey allows students to discover which Career Clusters and Pathways align with their preferences, and to guide their investigations and research. In doing so, they will have the opportunity to demonstrate application of the following skills:

College and Career Readiness Anchor Standards for Reading

Integration of Knowledge and Ideas (Reading Standards for Informational Text) – Grade 8

- Evaluate the advantages and disadvantages of using different mediums (e.g., print or digital text, video, multimedia) to present a particular topic or idea.

- Delineate and evaluate the argument and specific claims in a text, assessing whether the reasoning is sound and the evidence is relevant and sufficient; recognize when irrelevant evidence is introduced.

- Analyze a case in which two or more texts provide conflicting information on the same topic and identify where the texts disagree on matters of fact or interpretation.

Learning
Strategies

Use Summarizing and Note Taking to enhance students' ability to synthesize information and organize it in a way that captures the main ideas and supporting details.

The following are possible guiding questions: What are all possible sources for information about Career Clusters and personal interests and about trends for future impacts of technology in the workplace? Which are the best sources (accurate, authentic) that provide the information we need? How do we accurately summarize and cite the relevant information from the selected sources?

Critical Thinking,
Problem-Solving, &
Decision-Making

A. identify and define authentic problems and significant questions for investigation.

There is no more authentic or significant question than "What would be the best possible future I could create for myself?"

New idea: *Take Stock!* Students can use digital technologies to share and compare what they are learning about potential careers that best align with their interests, preferences, and goals, and let this information guide choices about course selection, service learning, and extracurricular activities. In doing so, they will have the opportunity to demonstrate application of the following skills:

College and Career Readiness Anchor Standards for Writing

Text Types and Purposes – Grade 8

- Write arguments to support claims in an analysis of substantive topics or texts, using valid reasoning and relevant and sufficient evidence.

- Write informative/explanatory texts to examine and convey complex ideas and information clearly and accurately through the effective selection, organization, and analysis of content.

- Write narratives to develop real or imagined experiences or events using effective technique, well-chosen details, and well-structured event sequences.

Learning
Strategies

Use Identifying Similarities and Differences to enhance students' understanding of and ability to use knowledge by engaging them in mental processes that involve identifying ways that Career Pathways are alike and different. Use a variety of information resources to determine which Career Cluster is a student's most and least favorite, in terms of providing direction for life after high

Digital
Citizenship

school.

C. demonstrate personal responsibility for lifelong learning.

By making presentations to peers, family, and the community, students make a powerful, positive statement about our collective hopes for the future. In doing so, they will have the opportunity to demonstrate application of the following skills:

Learning
Strategies

Use Reinforcing Effort and Providing Recognition to enhance students' understanding of the relationship between effort and achievement by addressing students' attitudes and beliefs about learning. Provide students with rewards or praise for their accomplishments related to producing a compelling presentation about examining how personal interests align with Career Clusters and related Career Pathways. Organize presentations for community groups and organizations for the most exemplary projects.

Technology
Operations &
Concepts

D. transfer current knowledge to learning of new technologies.

In many cases, researching, collaborating, and producing media-rich presentations will involve adding new tools and processes to students' repertoire.

Students document how this process worked, where there were successes and challenges, and how (and with whose help) those were overcome. In doing so, they will have the opportunity to demonstrate application of the following skills:

Learning
Strategies

Use Cues, Questions, and Advance Organizers to enhance students' ability to retrieve, use, and organize what they already know about a technology topic. Forecast the impact of technology changes for the Career Clusters students have picked as favorite and least favorite.

Appendix B

Multidisciplinary Project
Our Community Fifty Years from Now

Tom Carroll, president of the National Commission on Teaching and America's Future, has pointed out that teaching is the last "solo" profession where an individual is supposed to do everything singlehandedly (with the possible exception of goat herding). He further states that there are four ways to structure work:

1. Solo practice. People are expected to know and do everything on their own. As noted, this structure is still dominant in education; all other professions today use teams.

2. Artisan community. This is a group of people engaged in solo practice.

3. Guild. This is a professional community whose members share with each other, helping each other get better at solo practice.

4. Team. Teams have a single strategic goal and a game plan. They have an organization of staff that is differentiated and orchestrated around the plan. Team members practice the plan and assess their performance against the goal. There are two kinds of teams: independent teams (think Olympic figure skater team: they have a coach but perform individually) and interdependent teams (think

Olympic hockey team: no member can perform his task without depending on others to do their tasks).

Digital age learning challenges schools to change from teaching organizations to learning organizations, and this is simply not possible until we learn to work in teams. This multidisciplinary project provides a vehicle to travel that transitional space.

Sample Project: What Will Our Community Be Like in Fifty Years?

Let's take a look at how we can put together a multidisciplinary project that involves English, math, science, and geography in interlocking themes. The overarching theme is to have students project what they think our community might look like fifty years from now.

English

When we are looking into the future, we need also to see where we are right now, and this gives us a great opportunity to use digital storytelling. This component asks students to collaboratively explore information about our community history and prospects for the future, using that information in a variety of forms: poetry, websites, storytelling, video, and photography. In doing so, they will have the opportunity to demonstrate application of the following skills:

Math

Students are asked to project changes in the physical size of their community over the next fifty years based on population trends, using physical and digital models to demonstrate the underlying mathematical concepts. Modeling the future is more than simply adding up the number of people: some patterns of growth are linear (for each additional family, you're going to need one more house or apartment); some patterns are algebraic, because there are different numbers of children in each family. (Math Strands: numbers and operations, algebra, geometry) In meeting this challenge, they will have the opportunity to demonstrate application of the skills shown at right:

Science

Students use inquiry to identify factors to be considered in making informed decisions about land use and in deciding whether a new housing development will require building additional schools and, if necessary, where new schools should be built. (Science Strand: science in personal and social perspectives)

> **Common Core State Standards**
>
> *Mathematical Practices (Grade 8)*
>
> 1. Make sense of problems and persevere in solving them.
>
> 2. Reason abstractly and quantitatively.
>
> 3. Construct viable arguments and critique the reasoning of others.
>
> 4. Model with mathematics.
>
> 5. Use appropriate tools strategically.
>
> 6. Attend to precision.
>
> 7. Look for and make use of structure.
>
> 8. Look for and express regularity in repeated reasoning.

Geography

In this component, students create original data sets of locations in the community that they select, using tools such as a GPS or geographic information system (GIS); input spatial data into spreadsheets or databases; and then present findings using a variety of media. Some people can see trends by looking at tables of data, but most of us can't. And that's why we want to use nonlinguistic representation to show the story of the data. And in terms of research and information fluency, we're going to want to consult the pros. There are people in our communities who do this for their day jobs. Therefore, we want to divide the research process into two phases: first, find out what all the factors are; second, find out who all the experts are. Doing this with a team approach gives us the opportunity to hone our skills of cooperative learning.

College and Career Readiness Anchor Standards for Writing

Production and Distribution of Writing – Grade 8

- Produce clear and coherent writing in which the development, organization, and style are appropriate to task, purpose, and audience.

- Develop and strengthen writing as needed by planning, revising, editing, rewriting, or trying a new approach.

- Use technology, including the Internet, to produce and publish writing and to interact and collaborate with others.

Appendix C

How to Use the DVD

The DVD that accompanies this book contains three types of materials intended to help you implement the Digital Learning Process. These are Project Maps, resources, and video clips. All of these materials are contained in a PDF portfolio that you can open with Adobe Acrobat or Adobe Reader. I highly recommend that you update your Adobe Reader to the latest version for full functionality. You can download Adobe Reader for free from http://get.adobe.com/reader/.

When you insert the DVD into the DVD drive on your computer, you will see the following screen, in layout view, which is the default:

If you prefer, you can click on the detail view to see a listing of the files contained on the DVD.

Clicking on a file folder in either view brings you one level deeper into the content.

Core Subject Projects

Here is how the English projects appear, in layout view:

This is the same English project content in detail view. Note that hovering your cursor over the description area provides the full text of the project description.

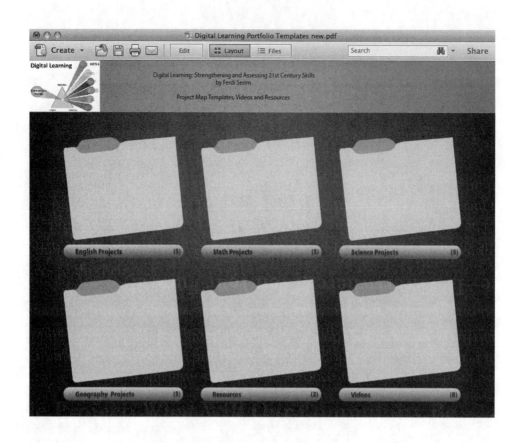

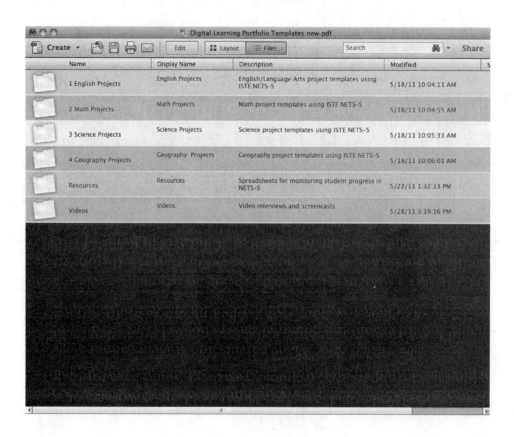

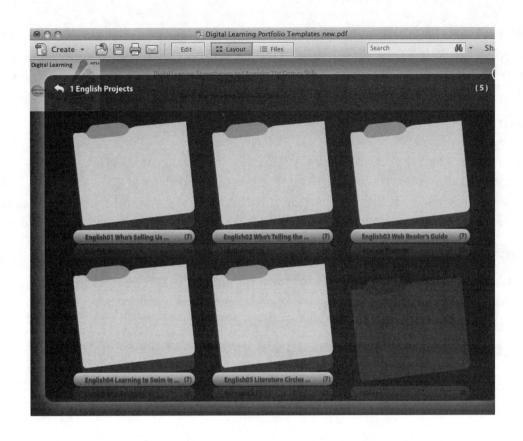

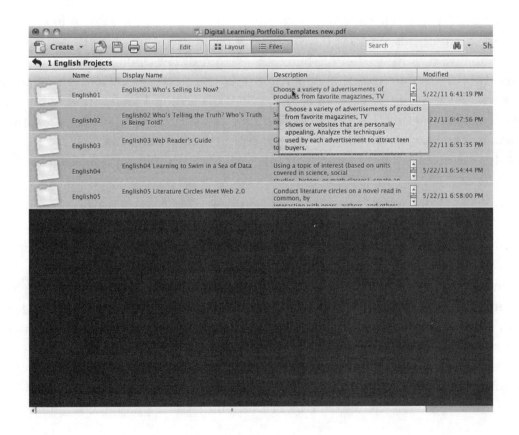

The organization of all four subjects (English, math, science, and geography) is identical. There is an "at a glance" file that describes the project as a whole, followed by Project Maps for each of the six ISTE NETS-S. This is why each project contains seven files.

Resources

I have included two spreadsheets for your use. The first, the Digital Learning Trends Template, contains no data and is ready for you to record your assessments of student progress against the NETS-S, as described in the text. The second spreadsheet contains sample data so that you can play with hypothetical information to get a feel for how the spreadsheet operates.

I have also included a survey for Technology Operations and Concepts, in Word version. The interactive version of this survey and a general Pre-Post Assessment of ISTE NETS-S (which allows you to compare your prior knowledge with what's expected of an 8th grader) are both available for free at the following Web addresses:

Pre-Assessment of Technology Operations & Concepts (NETS S6):

https://www.surveymonkey.com/s/NETS_S6_PreAssessment

PrePost ISTE NETS Survey for Students:

https://www.surveymonkey.com/s/PrePost_ISTE_NETSforStudents

I've included a spreadsheet that contains 165 Activity Types for TPACK in their respective academic areas. This allows you to align your technology choices with academic goals.

Additionally, a Word version of the Notes section of the book contains active hyperlinks to all of the resources cited. This list will be continually updated on del.icio.us at http://www.delicious.com/ferdiserim/bundle:DigitalLearning. Finally, the Digital Learning Process website is continually updated with new resources, strategies and best practices identified by educators implementing the process in their classrooms. You are encouraged to visit the site often, which is located at: http://digitallearningprocess.net/.

Videos

There are eight sets of video resources contained on the DVD; here is how they appear in layout view:

Switching to detail view allows you to see more information about each group of interviews and screencast videos.

Only QuickTime files version 2.0 or earlier can be played in Windows Media Player. Later versions of QuickTime require the proprietary Apple QuickTime Player. For more information, visit the following Apple Web site: http://www.apple.com/quicktime

For more information about any of the videos and the online course of which they are a part, visit http://www.kdsi.org/CL-Digital-Learning.aspx.

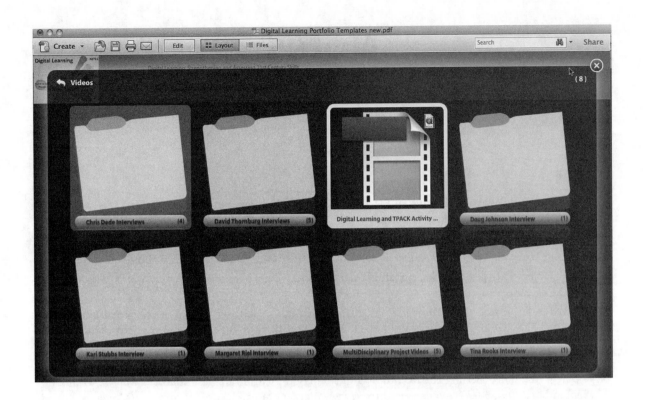

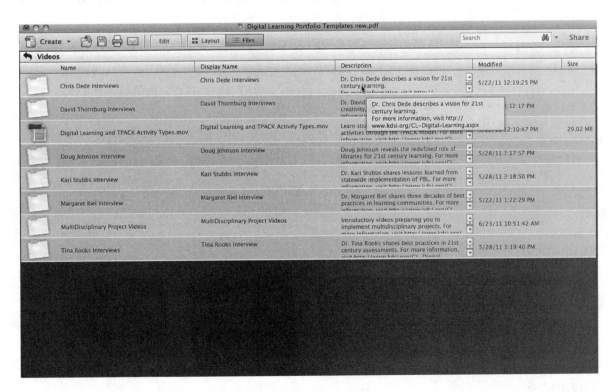

Notes

Chapter 1

1. Helen Barrett, "Pedagogical Issues in Electronic Portfolio Implementation," 2002, http://electronicportfolios.com/EPpedissues.pdf.
2. Wikipedia, "Andragogy," http://en.wikipedia.org/wiki/Andragogy.
3. Robyn R. Jackson, *Never Work Harder Than Your Students* (Alexandria, VA: ASCD, 2009).
4. Robert J. Marzano, Debra Pickering, and Jane E. Pollock, *Classroom Instruction That Works* (Alexandria, VA: ASCD, 2001).
5. Howard Pitler, Elizabeth R. Hubbell, Matt Kuhn, and Kim Malenoski, *Using Technology with Classroom Instruction That Works* (Alexandria, VA: ASCD, 2007). This book is available online at http://www.ascd.org/publications/books/107025.aspx. A PDF of *A Theory-Based Meta-Analysis of Research on Instruction* is available at http://www.mcrel.org/instructionmetaanalysis.
6. Robert J. Marzano, "Setting the Record Straight on High-Yield Strategies," *Phi Delta Kappan 91*, no. 6 (September 2009), 30–37. Available at http://www.marzanoresearch.com/documents/Marzano9-09.pdf.
7. Marzano, Pickering, and Pollock, *Classroom Instruction That Works*, 9.
8. Ibid.
9. Marzano, "Setting the Record Straight."
10. Ibid.
11. John Hattie, *Visible Learning: A Synthesis of over 800 Meta-Analyses Relating to Achievement* (New York: Routledge, 2009); Marzano, "Setting the Record Straight."
12. Judi Harris and Mark Hofer, "Instructional Planning Activity Types as Vehicles for Curriculum-Based TPACK Development," in *Research Highlights in Technology and Teacher Education 2009*, ed. Cleborne D. Maddux (Chesapeake, VA: Society for Information Technology in Teacher Education, 2009), 99–108. Available at http:activitytypes.wmwikis.net/file/view/HarrisHofer-TPACKActivityTypes.pdf.
13. Ibid.
14. Ibid.

Chapter 2

1. McREL, "Second-Order Change," Balanced Leadership Profile: Glossary Terms, https://www.educationleadershipthatworks.org/PopUp.aspx?pageMode=learningcenter&displayType=glossary&phrase=second-order%20change.
2. Helen Barrett, "Pedagogical Issues in Electronic Portfolio Implementation," 2002, http://electronicportfolios.com/EPpedissues.pdf.

Chapter 3

1. Intel, "Engaging Visual Learning," http://www.intel.com/about/corporateresponsibility/education/k12/tools.htm.
2. Rick DeFour, "Addressing Differences," December 3, 2009, www.allthingsplc.info/wordpress/?p=339.

Chapter 5

1. Mihaly Csikszentmihalyi, *Creativity: Flow and the Psychology of Discovery and Invention* (New York: HarperPerennial, 1996), 8.

2. Ibid., 23.

3. Ibid., 1.

4. Ibid., 11.

5. Helen Barrett, "Pedagogical Issues in Electronic Portfolio Implementation," 2002, http://electronicportfolios.com/EPpedissues.pdf.

6. Shepherd, Clive, "Assessing Your Communications Options," 1998. http://www.fastrak-consulting.co.uk/tactix/features/commopts/commopts.htm.

7. Wikipedia, "Longevity," http://en.wikipedia.org/wiki/Longevity.

8. Wikipedia, "Wicked Problem," http://en.wikipedia.org/wiki/Wicked_problem.

Chapter 6

1. SEIR*TEC, *Planning into Practice,* 2007, http://www.seirtec.org/plan/Ch%207.pdf.

2. Bruce Joyce and Beverley Showers, *Designing Training and Peer Coaching: Our Needs for Learning* (Alexandria, VA: ASCD, 2002).

Index

A

Abbott, E. A., 142
Access database (Microsoft), 57
Adobe Acrobat, 56, 169
Adobe Reader, 169
Affective networks, 25
Albemarle County, Virginia, 83
American Association of School Librarians, 99
American Memory Project, 28
Ames Research (NASA), 137
Analog age, 81
Andragogy, 4–6
Appalachia, 71
Are They Ready to Work? (Casner-Lotto and Brenner), 157
Artifacts, 41–43
Assessment Tool for Thinking (Creativity; *Intel Education K-12 Teaching Tools*), 46–47

B

"Ban Those Birds Units" (Loertscher), 99
Barrett, Helen, 2, 31, 41, 60
Benner, Mary Wright, 157
Bennis, Warren, 155
Best practices, rethinking for digital age, 23–32
"Big 5" modalities, 82
"Bird-watching" process, 37
Blanchard, M. R., 18
Blended model, power of, 48–50
"Blogs in Plain English" (TeacherTube), 55
Bubbl.Us, 54
Buck Institute for Education (BIE), 26

C

Career Clusters, 66, 118–119, 132; and connecting classroom and real life, 156–164; and employers' view of skill levels and high school students, 156–157; and English/Language Arts, 158–159; and Geography, 160–164; and highly developed core subject skills, 158–164; Interest Survey, 124, 158, 160; and Math, 159; and Pathways, 124–125, 132, 157, 158; and Science, 159–160
Carroll, Tom, 165
"Case for Instant Messaging in the Classroom, The" (Speedofcreativity.org), 56
Casner-Lotto, Jill, 157

CAST. *See* Center for Applied Special Technologies (CAST)
Center for Applied Special Technologies (CAST), 24, 60
Center for Technology in Learning (SRI International), 30
Change, as bringing danger and opportunity, 22
CityMayors Website, 144
Classroom 2.0 (online resource), 54, 55
Classroom Assessment and Grading That Work (Marzano), 12
Classroom Instruction That Works (Marzano, Pickering, and Pollock), 12
Classroom Management That Works (Marzano, Pickering, and Marzano), 12
Cloud, the, 56
Cmap tools, 34
Collaborative online learning, five elements of leadership for (Riel), 50–52
College and Career Readiness Anchor Standards for Reading, 8; Integration of Knowledge and Ideas (Reading Standards for Informational Text)-Grade 8, 73, 88, 89, 105, 107, 114, 128, 161; Key Ideas and Details (Reading Standards for Informational Text)-Grade 8, 88, 106
College and Career Readiness Anchor Standards for Writing: Production and Distribution of Writing-Grade 8, 72, 74, 115, 117, 129, 161, 163, 168; Research to Build and Present Knowledge-Grade 8, 73, 87, 104, 116, 130, 160, 167; Text Types and Purposes-Grade 8, 162
College and Career Ready standards, 5, 6
Common Core State Standards, 7, 8, 10, 16, 28
Common Core State Standards- Mathematical Practices (Grade 8), 75, 76, 90, 108, 109, 119, 132, 167
Common Core State Standards-Math Grade 8: Expressions and Equations-8.EE, 91, 133; Functions-8.F, 91, 109, 118, 119; Statistics and Probability-8.SP, 75, 90
Common Craft, 54
Communication and Collaboration standard (NETS-S2), 2–3, 9, 71–85; and assessing collaboration, 85; and assessing communication, 85; challenge of, for students in English, 72–74; challenge of, for students in Geography, 79–81; challenge of, for students in Math, 75–76; challenge of, for students in Science, 76–78; and communications, then and now, 81–82;

and communications dimensions, in general, 82; with high-probability strategies, 84–85; and keeping pace with emerging technologies, 82–84; Serim's theorems on, 81

Concept Draw, 34

Content creation tools, 56

Cooperative learning, 61–62, 72, 73, 76, 78–80, 96, 97, 105, 108, 135, 145

Council of Chief State School Officers, 7

Creativity: assessing, 46–47; closer look at, 59–60; and Creativity 101 for educators, 60; designing for, 60; and judgment, 48; risk-taking and, 47–48

Creativity (Csikszentmihalyi), 59

Creativity and Innovation standard (NETS-S1), 2, 9, 35, 39, 59–70; assessing, 69–70; challenge of, for students in English, 61–62; challenge of, for students in Geography, 68–70; challenge of, for students in Math, 63–65; challenge of, for students in Science, 66–67

Critical thinking, 83, 103

Critical Thinking, Problem Solving, and Decision Making standard (NETS-S4), 3, 9, 41, 103–112; assessing, 112; challenge of, for students in English, 104–107; challenge of, for students in Math, 108–110; challenge of, for students in Science, 110–112

CSI (television series), 150

Csikszentmihalyi, Mihaly, 59–60

Cues, Questions, and Advance Organizers, 68, 90, 92, 128, 130–134, 137, 144, 164

D

Data management tools, 56–57

Dede, Chris, 23; on connected teaching model, 21–22; on the need to aim high, 21

Del.icio.us, 172

Design and Develop Digital-Age Learning Experiences and Assessments teacher standard-NETS-T2, 146–148; and insights on 21st century assessment (Rooks), 147–148

Digital age learning: and assessing creativity, 46–47; "look fors" of, 46–47; rethinking, 23–32; roadmap to success with, 9–20; why now? why me?, 1–22

Digital age teaching and learning tool kit, 53–57; and anytime and real-time communication and collaboration tools, 54–56; and anytime communication tools, 55; and content creation tools, 56; and data management tools, 56–57; and Google Earth, GPS, and GIS tools, 57; and real-time communication tools, 55–56

Digital Citizenship (NETS-S5), 3, 113–126; assessing, 126; challenge of, for students in English, 115–117; challenge of, for students in Geography, 123–125; challenge of, for students in Math, 118–120; challenge of, for students in Science, 121–122; recommended activity for: Project Speak Up, 125

Digital Learning activity types: and English activity (E01), 35, 44; and Geography Activity Type, 79; and Geography Activity Type: Convergent Knowledge

Expression (Engage in Data-Based Inquiry), 98, 123, 124, 136; and Geography Activity Type: Knowledge Building (Compare and Contrast), 96, 124; and Geography Activity Type: Knowledge Building (Engage in Artifact-Based Inquiry), 97; and Geography Activity Type: Knowledge Building (Engage in Data-Based Inquiry), 97; and Science Activity Type: Conceptual Knowledge Building (Data Analysis), 93, 122, 134, 136, 138; and Science Activity Type: Conceptual Knowledge Building (Develop Predictions, Hypotheses, Questions, Variables), 110; and Science Activity Type: Knowledge Expression (Debate), 95, 121; and Science Activity Type: Knowledge Expression (Do a Presentation or Demonstration), 94; and Science Activity Type: Knowledge Expression (Do a Presentation/ Demonstration, Debate), 112; and Science Activity Type: Procedural Knowledge Building (Observe, Collect Samples, Do Procedures, Record Data), 111, 135; and Science Activity Type: Procedural Knowledge Building (Record Data), 94, 122

Digital Learning Process, 1, 2; and collaborative online learning, 50–52; and Digital Learning Process Prism: making things visible, 33–34; and Digital Learning Trends spreadsheet, 36–41; guiding growth and generating evidence in, 41–45; and "look fors" of digital age learning, 46–48; and power of blended model, 48–50; and providing guidance, 45–46; research basis for, 14–21; and Technological, Pedagogical, and Content Knowledge (TPACK) model, 15–16; using graphical organizers in, 34–41

Digital Learning Project Maps, 4, 7, 29–30; as framework for skill development and assessment, 10–11

Digital Learning Trends spreadsheet, 146, 149; and differentiating according to need, 37–38; and measuring for growth, 39; and student ownership, 39–41; using, 36–41

Digital Learning Trends Template, 172

Digital natives, 53, 84

Diigo tool, 54

Down the Drain project, 63, 119

Dr. Kildare (television show), 150

Driving question, writing, 28–29

drop.io (file-sharing tool), 54

DVD, using, 169; core subject projects on, 169–172

E

Edison, Thomas, 82

EDUCAUSE, 82

EDUCAUSE Learning Initiative (ELI), 82–83

Einstein, Alfred, 47, 105

ELI. *See* EDUCAUSE Learning Initiative (ELI)

Elluminate (editing tool), 56

Emerging technologies, keeping pace with, 82–84

Energy Efficiency and Renewable Energy (U.S. Department of Energy), 108

Engage in Professional Growth and Leadership teacher standard (NETS-T5), 153–155

English activity (E01), 35; goals of, 44
English/Language Arts, 158–159
Enhancing Education Through Technology (EETT), 139
ePals, 28, 73, 80, 123, 145
ESSPs. *See* NSF Earth System Science Projects
Etherpad (editing tool), 56
Evaluation, 43–44
Evidence, generating, 41–45

F

Facilitate and Inspire Student Learning and Creativity
  teacher standard (NETS-T1), 144–145
Flatland: A Romance of Many Dimensions (Abbott), 142
Four D's (Project-Based Learning): and debrief phase
  (fourth D), 31; and define phase (first D), 26; and
  design phase (second D), 29–30; and do phase (third
  D), 30–31
FreeMind, 34
Frontline (PBS), 7, 36, 43, 44, 46

G

Generating and Testing Hypotheses, 104, 106–109, 111,
  112
GenYES model, 138–139
Geographic information system (GIS)tools, 57, 68, 96,
  136, 168
Geography, 160–164
Geography Activity Type, 96; Convergent Knowledge
  Expression, Visual Divergent Knowledge Expression,
  79, 80; Knowledge Building, 79; Visual Divergent
  Knowledge Expression, 80
Gibson, William, 53
Gifted and Talented programs, 60
GIS tools. *See* Geographic information system (GIS)tools
Global Learning and Observations to Benefit the
  Environment (GLOBE), 137
GlobalSchoolNet, 28, 80, 123
GLOBE. *See* Global Learning and Observations to Benefit
  the Environment (GLOBE)
Google, 86
Google Docs, 56, 83
"Google Docs in Plain English" (TeacherTube), 55
Google Earth, 54, 57, 79; Blog, 57
Google Maps, 79
GPS, 57, 168
Graphical organizers, 34–41; and project maps, 35–36;
  and types of software available, 34
Grey's Anatomy (television series), 150
Growth, guiding, 41–45; and artifacts, 41–43; and
  evaluation, 43–44; and reflections, 43; and validation,
  44–45
Guidance, providing, 45–46
"Guide to Using Elluminate" (Classroom 2.0), 55

H

H2O for Life, 95, 110
Harris, Judi, 15–18, 20

Hattie, John, 14, 48
Hofer, Mark, 15–18, 20
Homework and Practice, 89, 133, 136, 138
"How to Lie with Statistics" (Web page), 63, 75, 118
Hubbell, Elizabeth R., 11

I

iCHAT, 145
ICT. *See* Information, Communications, and Technology
  (ICT) Literacy, definition of
Identifying Similarities and Differences, 63, 64, 67–69, 88,
  89, 117, 138, 145, 162
In Plain English (TeacherTube and YouTube), 54
Individuals with Disabilities Education Act (IDEA)
  funding, 60
Information, Communications, and Technology (ICT)
  Literacy, 118–119, 132; definition of, 100
Information fluency, insights on (Johnson), 98–100
Inspiration (software), 34, 35, 45
"Instant Messaging" (Classroom 2.0), 55
Integration of Knowledge and Ideas standard (College
  and Career Readiness Anchor Standards for Reading), 8
Intel Education K-12 Teaching Tools, 46–48
Intel Teach Assessment library, 69–70
Intellectual property, 61
International Society for Technology in Education
  (ISTE), 2
ISTE. *See* International Society for Technology in
  Education (ISTE)

J

Johnson, Doug, 98–100
Joyce, Bruce, 154
Judgment, 48

K

Kapp, Alexander, 5
Kathy Schrock's Web 2.0 Tools (online resource), 54
Kidspiration, 34
Knowledge Building, 17, 31, 86
Knowledge Expression, 17
Knowles, Malcolm, 5
Kuhn, Matt, 11

L

Last Book in the Universe, The (Philbrick), 61, 87
Leadership Institute (University of Southern California),
  155
Learning Circles (Riehl), 30, 31, 150, 153
Lefever, Lee, 54
Loertscher, D., 99

M

Malenoski, Kim, 11
Mankato Public Schools (Minnesota), 98–100
Marketing Career Cluster, 157
Marzano, J. S., 12

Marzano, Robert, 10, 39, 84, 86; and digital use of high-probability strategies, 13–14; high-probability instructional strategies of, 11–13; and student self-reporting, 14

Math, 159

Math Activity Types, 18

McREL. *See* Mid-continent Research for Education and Learning (McREL)

Mentorship, 154

"Merchants of Cool, The" (PBS *Frontline*), 7

Microsoft Office, 57

Mid-continent Research for Education and Learning (McREL), 11, 26

Model Digital-Age Work and Learning teacher standard (NETS-T3), 149–150

Model the Future (Thornburg; video interview transcript), 64–65

Multidisciplinary project, 165–168; and English, 166–167; and Geography, 168; and Math, 167; sample, 166–168; and Science, 167

N

NASA, 137

National Commission on Teaching and America's Future, 165

National Educational Technology Plan, 22

National Educational Technology Standards for Students (NETS-S; International Society for Technology in Education), 2–4, 6, 16, 35; and Communication and Collaboration standard (NETS-S2), 2–3, 9, 71–85; and Creativity and Innovation standard (NETS-S1), 2, 9, 35, 39, 59–70; and Critical Thinking, Problem Solving, and Decision Making standard (NETS-S4), 3, 9, 41, 103–112; and Digital Citizenship standard (NETS-S5), 3, 9, 113–126; and Research and Information Fluency standard (NETS-S3), 3, 9, 45, 86–102; and Technology Operations and Concepts (NETS-S6), 4, 9, 127–140

National Educational Technology Standards for Teachers (NETS-T; International Society for Technology in Education), 6, 141–155; and Design and Develop Digital-Age Learning Experiences and Assessments standard (NETS-T2), 146–148; and Engage in Professional Growth and Leadership standard (NETS-T5), 153–155; and Facilitate and Inspire Student Learning and Creativity standard (NETS-T1), 144–145; and Model Digital-Age Work and Learning standard (NETS-T3), 149–150; and Promote and Model Digital Citizenship and Responsibility (NETS-T4), 151–152

National Geographic, 71

National Governors Association Center for Best Practices, 7

National Oceanic and Atmospheric Administration, 137

New Mexico, 13, 57

New Mexico Media Literacy Project, 45–46

Nick at Nite (television series), 81

Ning (social network), 54

Ninja Turtles (television), 150

No Child Left Behind (NCLB), 4, 147

Nonlinguistic Representation, 63, 66, 73, 75, 77, 80, 109, 123

Northwest Regional Educational Laboratory, 139

NSF Earth System Science Projects (ESSPs), 137

O

"100 Web Tools for Every Kind of Learner" (Collegeathome.com), 56

Ozzie and Harriet (television series), 6, 81

P

Partnership for 21st Century Skills Information and Communication Technologies (ICT), 4

Partnership for 21st Century Skills Information and Communication Technologies (ICT)map, 7, 10, 27

PBL. *See* Project-based learning (PBL)

PBL Do It Yourself page (BIE), 26

PBL Starter Kit (Buck Institute for Education), 26–29, 31

PBS. *See* Public Broadcasting Service (PBS)

Pedagogical content knowledge, 16

Pedagogy, 4

Peer review, 39; guidelines for, 40–41

Perry Mason (television series), 150

Philbrick, Rodman, 61, 87

Pickering, D. J., 12

PISA. *See* Programme for International Student Assessment (PISA) ICT

Pitler, Howard, 11

PlayStation, 61–62, 87

Pollock, J. E., 12

PowerPoint, 34, 126

Product Oriented Divergent Knowledge Expression activities, 17

Professional Development (PD), 154

Programme for International Student Assessment (PISA) ICT, 100; Framework for Assessing ICT Literacy: Integrating, Constructing, and Communicating Information, 163

Project Maps, 35–36, 41, 45

Project Speak Up, 125

Project-based learning (PBL): and empowering students and teachers, 26; and four D's, 26–31

Promote and Model Digital Citizenship and Responsibility teacher standard (NETS-T4), 151–152

Public Broadcasting Service (PBS), 7

R

Recognition networks, 25

Reflections, 43

Reinforcing Effort and Providing Recognition, 95, 115, 116, 118, 120–122, 124, 163

Research and Information Fluency standard(NETS-S3), 3, 9, 45, 86–102; assessing, 101–102; challenge of, for students in English, 87–89; challenge of, for students in Geography, 96–98; challenge of, for students in Math, 90–92; challenge of, for students in Science,

93–95; and insights on information fluency (Johnson), 98–100; and moving from content experts to process experts, 98–99; and redefining research, 99–100

Resources, 172

Riel, Margaret, 30, 31, 50, 58, 150, 153

Risk-taking, 47–48

Rooks, Tina, 147–148

S

Santa Fe, New Mexico, 48

Schneider, Steven, 139

Schrock, Kathy, 54

Science, Technology, Engineering and Mathematics (STEM) professionals, 50, 66, 159

Science Activity Types, 18, 93–95, 121

Science Learning Activity Types (Blanchard, Harris, and Hofer), 18

Secondary English Language Arts, 19–20

Secondary English Language Arts Learning Activity Types (Young, Hofer, and Harris), 19–20

Serim, Ferdi, 21; theorems of, on Communication and Collaboration, 81

Setting Objectives and Providing Feedback, 129, 133, 135, 137

"7 Things You Should Know About" (EDUCAUSE), 82

Shakespeare, William, 61–62, 87

Showers, Beverly, 154

Skype, 56, 106, 145

"Skype: Using Videoconferencing to Enhance Learning" (Classroom 2.0), 55

Smartdraw, 34

Social Studies Activity Types, 17

Sony, 61–62, 87

SRI International, 30

Strategic networks, 25

SubEthaEdit, 83

Summarizing and Note Taking, 76, 77, 91, 93, 94, 97, 98, 162

T

TeacherTube, 54, 55, 153

Team collaboration, 83

Technological, Pedagogical, and Content Knowledge (TPACK), 15–16, 86, 157, 172

Technological content knowledge, 16

Technological pedagogical knowledge, 16

Technology Operations and Concepts standard (NETS-S6), 4, 127–140; assessing, 140; challenge of, for students in English, 128–131; challenge of, for students in Geography, 136–139; challenge of, for students in Math, 132–133; challenge of, for students in Science, 134–136; and leveraging untapped expertise: GenYES

model, 138–139; Pre-Assessment of, 172; PrePost ISTE NETS Survey for Students, 172; survey for, 172

TechYES project, 138–139

Theory Based Meta-Analysis of Research on Instruction (McREL), 11

Think.com, 28

Thornburg, David, 64, 142

Tommorrow.org, 125

TPACK. *See* Technological, Pedagogical, and Content Knowledge (TPACK)

Turning Technologies, 147

U

United Nations, 104

Universal design for learning, 24–25; and three sets of characteristics shared by expert learners, 24

University of Southern California (USC), 155

U.S. Census Bureau, 104

U.S. Department of Energy, 108

Using Technology with Classroom Instruction That Works (Pitler, Hubbell, Kuhn, and Malenoski), 11

V

Validation, 44–45

Vanishing Videos forensic problem-solving activity (wiredsafety.org), 105, 106

Videos, 172

Visual learning techniques, 33; four key benefits to students of, 33–34

Voice over Internet Protocol (VoIP), 55

W

Web 2.0 technologies, 22, 54, 72, 82

White, Paula, 83–84

Who's Selling Us Now? (Digital Learning Project), 7–10, 27–31, 58

"Wicked problems," 112

Wikis, 83–84

"Wikis in Plain English" (TeacherTube), 55

WiredSafety, 113

Wolinsky, Art, 105, 113

Woodside Research Consortium, 139

WorldWind (NASA), 137

Y

Young, C. A., 20

"Your Three Brain Networks" activity (CAST), 25

YouthCaN, 80, 123

YouTube, 29, 85; "RSS Feeds in Plain English," 54

Z

Zoho Creator, 57